THE COMPLETE CEO

THE COMPLETE CEO

The Executive's Guide to Consistent Peak Performance

Mark Thomas

with Gary Miles and Peter Fisk

CAPSTONE

Copyright © 2006 PA Knowledge Ltd
The right of Mark Thomas, Gary Miles and Peter Fisk to be identified as the
authors of this book has been asserted in accordance with the Copyright,
Designs and Patents Act 1988

First published 2006 by
Capstone Publishing Limited (a Wiley Company)
The Atrium
Southern Gate
Chichester
West Sussex
PO19 8SQ
www.wileyeurope.com
Email (for orders and customer service enquires): cs-books@wiley.co.uk

Designations used by companies to distinguish their products are often claimed
as trademarks. All brand names and product names used in this book are trade
names, service marks, trademarks or registered trademarks of their respective
owners. The Publisher is not associated with any product or vendor mentioned
in this book.

This publication is designed to provide accurate and authoritative information
in regard to the subject matter covered. It is sold on the understanding that the
Publisher is not engaged in rendering professional services. If professional advice
or other expert assistance is required, the services of a competent professional
should be sought.

CIP catalogue records for this book are available from the British Library and the
US Library of Congress

ISBN-13: 978-1-84112-728-6
ISBN-10: 1-84112-728-0

Typeset in 10/14pt Merdien by Sparks, Oxford – www.sparks.co.uk
Printed and bound in Great Britain by TJ International Ltd, Padstow, Cornwall

This book is printed on acid-free paper responsibly manufactured from sustainable forestry in which at least two trees are planted for each one used for paper
production.

For all those who have dedicated themselves to the ultimately impossible, but infinitely rewarding, task of being a complete CEO.

Contents

Foreword

That CEOs should perform well is of the utmost importance to society. Companies that perform well, sustainably, generate huge value for their customers, fulfilment for their staff and, of course, attractive returns for their shareholders; and it is their CEOs who are ultimately responsible for making sure that companies do perform. Unfortunately, the world conspires to make it increasingly difficult to guarantee such performance. In most industries today, there is overcapacity; many are facing unprecedented global competition; and in many sectors, products are commoditizing faster than ever before.

In essence, despite these challenges, the job of being a CEO is a simple one: the CEO has to do three things well: to set the tone, to get the right people in place and to set the agenda. Setting the agenda is clear: where the CEO focuses will be where the organization focuses – and it falls to the CEO to make sure that the most painful realities as well as the most important opportunities are addressed. Getting the right people in place is also self-evident: no CEO can do much alone. The tone is the hardest: as CEO, one sets a tone without even thinking about it: the people one spends time with; one's pace of work and decision-making; one's extravagance or frugality – all send powerful signals into the organization, and the response to these signals can make a material difference over time to the health of the business.

Though it may be simple, it is difficult to get these things right, and this is where *The Complete CEO* has made a courageous effort, for the first time, to spell out what CEOs have to do to be successful. The high-performance model, at the core of the book, moves from a clear and insightful discussion of what drives the creation and maintenance of a winning business model into a decomposition of the role of the CEO. The authors have worked with a number of highly successful CEOs and former CEOs to understand the essence of their success, and the actions they have taken day-to-day to drive it, and the result is a practical, easy-to-understand guide.

Of course, the raw material is the most important ingredient in making a successful CEO, but I believe that any new CEO, or indeed manager of a business unit, who takes seriously the challenges set out in this book, and makes wise use of the tools and techniques it suggests, will find ways to improve his or her performance.

Ben Verwaayen, CEO BT Group

Acknowledgements

As this book was approaching its completion, we started to set down the names of those who had helped us in writing it, and were astonished at the length of the list.

First and foremost, we must thank those CEOs who have worked with us, informed us and inspired us and on whose insights most of this book is based. Many of these CEOs are profiled or quoted extensively within the text: Warren Buffett, Chairman of Berkshire Hathaway; Michael Critelli, CEO of Pitney Bowes; Gareth Davies, CEO of Imperial Tobacco; Mervyn Davies, CEO of Standard Chartered Bank, who provided us with extraordinary detail about his early days in charge; Mike Frayne, Chairman of Intec Telecom; Justin King, CEO of Sainsbury's; Michael Krasny, former CEO of CDW; John McGrath, former CEO of Diageo and then Chairman of Boots; Tim Parker, CEO of the AA; Sir Brian Pitman, former Chairman and Chief Executive of Lloyds TSB; Ben Verwaayen, CEO of British Telecom – to whom we owe a special debt of gratitude for the foreword; and Joseph Wan, CEO of Harvey Nichols.

In addition to those we quoted were a number of CEOs with whom we have worked closely and who helped enormously by commenting on the concepts and drafts of the book but who out of an exaggerated sense of modesty declined to be profiled: Rolf Börjesson, CEO and now Chairman of Rexam; Jim Nicol, CEO of Tomkins; Sten Scheibye, the Chief Executive of Coloplast; and Terry Twigger, CEO of Meggitt.

To all of these we are extremely grateful. Another group whose untiring support was essential to the completion of this book were our colleagues. Matt Smith deserves special mention for his stamina: he has been involved from the conception of the book through to its completion. The PA Information Services Group, led by Sarah Wilkins, has worked tirelessly to provide us with the information we needed to illustrate the points in the book. James Allen, Sarah Cochrane, Murray Horrex, Lavinia Pickles, Annabel Pritchard, Selina Scales, Natalie Skidmore, Will Stevens and Robert Verwaayen have all made invaluable contributions to various sections. We are also grateful to our own CEO, Bruce Tindale, for his support for the project.

Paul Bradford, Khosrow Eghtesadi and Rae Sedel deserve thanks for introducing us to CEOs we have profiled.

The book has also benefited enormously from the critique of professional writers: Jim O'Loughlin made a number of insightful comments which helped us restructure an early draft, Richard Heller took a later draft and helped us to improve readability and Steve Coomber has laboured mightily to make the book look like a book rather than a consulting report.

Finally, thanks must go to our publishers, John Moseley and Mark Allin, for their extraordinary patience and understanding as we worked and reworked the manuscript.

Who is this book for?

Despite the title, this book is not just for CEOs. Yes, it is written for all those executives on the way to the boardroom and the position of chief executive officer, as well as for those already there – and for anyone interested in what the CEO does and should do to become an effective and successful CEO, and help build a great company. But, and this is an important point, this book is also written for a much wider audience. If you are a divisional or functional head, in charge of a strategic business unit or a corporate group, even a team, or if you aspire to any of these positions, then this book is for you.

Introduction

In charge of some of the major forces shaping society, the CEOs of the twenty-first century bear an enormous weight of responsibility. Their role is a difficult and challenging one. They are faced with a barrage of challenges that test their abilities to the extreme. Globalization means that business is more complex and competitive; customers are more demanding; there is growing pressure from financial institutions to meet performance expectations; change management and restructuring are high on the boardroom agenda; talented personnel are in short supply; and the pace of technological change, particularly the use of information technology, continues to accelerate. Plus, there is increased scrutiny from a variety of audiences and stakeholders including the media, NGOs, shareholders, customers and employees.

The demands of running a corporation create contradictory pressures. CEOs are routinely expected to make quick decisions while keeping a long-term perspective and to reconcile the imperative for performance with ethical concerns and questions of corporate responsibility.

Warren Bennis of the University of Southern California, and one of the world's leading authorities on leadership, believes the CEO's job is tougher than it has ever been:

> The job is more complex. There's a more clogged cartography of stakeholders, unbelievable changes, disruptive technologies, globalization, inflection points no one would even think ten years ago, and most of all, speed. It not only takes a strong stomach

and a tough nervous system but a mind that can take nine points of view and connect the dots.

On one hand the modern CEO is expected to be modest, unpretentious, engaging, flexible, diplomatic, ethical certainly, even humble. Yet that same person is expected to deal confidently with a rapacious media, boldly carry off audacious deals and fearlessly take on competitors. Truly great CEOs, it seems, require a perplexing combination of apparently incompatible characteristics.

CEO school?

So how do CEOs prepare for this onerous task? Is there a CEO school where future CEOs hone their skills? Unfortunately not. There are no CEO training schools; there are no standard examinations; not even a textbook. Rarely have we seen a decent job description.

The hands-on role of the CEO is a much misunderstood topic. Most CEOs learn from exposure to their own bosses – twenty years of absorption from a variety of CEOs, supplemented perhaps by an early spell at business school and combined, hopefully, with a pinch of natural talent. Global industry truly trusts to luck when it places an untrained CEO in position.

We decided that the role of CEO should be a mystery no longer. We plan to explode the myth, and portray the reality. In this book we provide a comprehensive taxonomy of the role of CEO. Each aspect of the CEO's role is explored in detail.

Our taxonomy is based on a series of our own models and tools, well established through many years of consulting work. These models have been developed and tested with a group of some of the most successful CEOs of the last twenty years – successful as recorded by what we believe is the one true success measure, long-term total shareholder return (but more of that later). Extensive interviews with these CEOs reveal a tale of ordered simplicity and care. Our research shows that great CEOs are great because of adherence to high personal standards, simple principles, common-sense rules and an inexhaustible curiosity. Our CEOs are not film stars, TV personalities or superheroes – though they are of course very talented. We conclude that the route to being a successful CEO is open to more people than is commonly thought.

Being a successful CEO is about more than total shareholder return though. Being a CEO means judging your own behaviour – and rewards – against the standards you want your company to observe. Being a CEO gives you a responsibility that goes beyond your formal legal and fiduciary duties. It means looking after the welfare of something bigger than yourself. If you are not up for this responsibility, do not bother to read the rest.

There are many books on management. Hundreds, if not thousands. Most seek to illuminate a single area such as leadership or strategy; or else they tell the story of a particular CEO or business. Few, however, get their hands dirty and actually dissect and examine what the CEO does and should do. This book is not a skim through the soft skills of leadership, although it does address some of these issues where relevant. It is a tough, realistic look at the nuts and bolts of the CEO's job. It contains valuable practical advice and a high-performance model that can be applied in real life. It provides a comprehensive framework – and is in this sense 'complete'.

Some highly successful CEOs have told us that the principles, guidelines and tools contained in this book have proved extremely useful in their day-to-day work of leading a successful organization. We trust that you will find them useful too.

Our research

The authors have had the immense privilege of working with some of the most successful CEOs in North America and northern Europe, both in the preparation of this book and in our day-to-day consulting activities. These CEOs have all produced real value for their shareholders. Most of the valuable insights in these pages have come from these executives, and our debt to them is immense. We have also had the opportunity to conduct systematic research with 1,000 leaders of the world's largest quoted companies over the period 1997–2005. By comparing the ways these leaders ran their businesses with their long-term performance, we have been able to distil some valuable lessons about what works in practice. Again, our debt to these leaders is enormous.

Overview

Many people aspire to be a CEO. They want to perform well, and have every reason to believe that they have the ability.

Once they are appointed, they find that the job has unique challenges. On any realistic measure of performance, about half of all CEOs fail.

How can you be one of the successes?

You might simply be lucky. You may make one decision that brings spectacular rewards. If you are a publisher, you might decide to publish the first *Harry Potter*; or if you are in movies, to produce the first *Star Wars*. Or your hapless predecessor as CEO may have made a decision that makes your results look good. But it is unwise to bet on your luck – and not many investors will do so without solid evidence that you know what you are doing.

This book argues that the fundamental purpose of any CEO is to maximize long-term shareholder value, which entails making an economic profit – paying back investors for the capital tied up in the business. Alarmingly, we found that over half of the companies worldwide that we researched have no idea whether they are achieving this at company level, still less at product or divisional level. Without such a measure, the CEOs of these companies are lucky if they manage to deliver.

Analysis of the best-performing CEOs shows that you can greatly increase your chances of success by mastering the four key levels of the CEO role (see Figure 1).

The book will help you to master each of these levels:

- The fundamentals: building the foundations – understanding clearly and committing to the challenge of long-term success

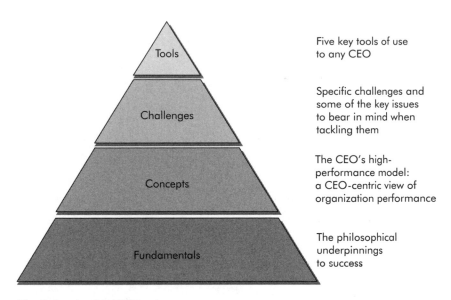

Fig. 1 Levels of the CEO role.
Source: PA analysis.

- Key concepts: applying the CEO's high-performance model to managing your business

- In practice: addressing the challenges you face with a constant focus on long-term shareholder value, despite the inherent distractions

- The CEO toolkit: making use of a number of proven CEO tools to help you apply the model.

In order to address these four levels, the book is split into four corresponding parts.

Part 1

The Fundamentals of Success

This first part of the book sets the context for the rest. It defines a number of concepts on which the rest of the book depends:

- Section 1 looks at the fundamental question of what is success for a CEO and concludes that CEOs are judged against far more demanding standards than most other managers. It demonstrates that long-term success for CEOs is synonymous with long-term shareholder value creation by their organizations. It explains that delivering long-term shareholder value requires the ability to create value for all direct stakeholders in the organization – most particularly for customers – and to motivate managers and staff to improve continually: a stiff set of challenges.

- Section 2 looks at some of the CEOs who have been most successful over the last ten years, and notes the extraordinary variety of styles and actions which led to that success. There appear to be no silver bullets either in terms of style or actions.

- Section 3 defines two of the key roles of the CEO: management and leadership. Broadly, management means making good decisions, and leadership means acting to ensure that your whole organization carries those decisions out. These two are quite different; they are both necessary, but neither on its own is sufficient. To be successful, a CEO has to work out how he or she will do both. Almost inevitably this involves recognizing and neutralizing some areas of personal weakness.

1 What is success for the CEO?

There is a continuing and lively debate about the ultimate purpose of a business. Some claim that the overarching purpose of a business is to ensure its own long-term survival. Others argue that a business exists in order to serve its customers, to preserve employment or to serve society more widely. Many managers believe that their job is to grow profits, or even just the size of the business. Finally, there is a school of thought that says that the job of managers is to maximize the long-term value of the business to its owners, the shareholders.

While this debate is entertaining, perhaps it does not matter all that much, since all the proposed objectives are mutually dependent. For example, a business that fails to keep its customers happy over a protracted period will not remain profitable (unless it is a monopoly): maintaining at least a reasonable level of customer satisfaction is essential for long-term financial success. Similarly, without the ability to attract and retain good staff, it becomes very difficult to sustain customer satisfaction.

In fact, if the shareholders are to benefit, it seems all the other stakeholders must be satisfied. So maybe the ultimate purpose of the business is unimportant; maybe all these different purposes for business are, in fact, equally important.

But this is emphatically not the case. The purposes outlined above are *not equivalent*. Far from it. While it *is* true that customer satisfaction is *necessary* to sustain an attractive level of financial performance, it does not follow that it is *sufficient*. A good example is the air transport industry.

Despite all our grumbles, this has provided a valuable service to millions of satisfied business customers and holidaymakers. Yet, since the Second World War, the industry as a whole has struggled to turn a profit.

If size, growth, ability to satisfy customers, ability to provide employment, and ability to support a large supplier base were measures of business success, the air transport industry would score very highly – but from a financial perspective it is a disaster. Many of its major players survive in their current form only because of government subsidies and protection from commercial realities. At the time of writing, for example, three of the leading five airlines in the US – United Airlines, Delta and Northwest – were operating under Chapter 11 bankruptcy protection.

Different purposes lead businesses in different directions. As CEO, it is vital to be crystal clear about your definition of success, because the rest of the organization will follow your lead. What *you define* as success internally will set the direction for the company and will determine whether in ten years' time, the business you are running resembles a loss-making airline or a company like Warren Buffet's Berkshire Hathaway in the US, which has returned a 24-plus annual return to its shareholders for well over four decades.

This section explains why maximizing the long-term shareholder value of the business must be the overarching goal of a company. CEOs are perceived as successful if, and only if, they perform against this measure. In fact, the successful CEO has to deliver long-term shareholder value regardless of any other ambitions:

- For the CEO, success must stand for the *success of the business*, not for a measure of personal contribution

- Whatever else is achieved, the CEO must get the business to deliver shareholder value

- Creating shareholder value entails making an economic profit – paying back the capital tied up in the business – something that many CEOs fail to measure and understand

- Shareholder value can be helped by pursuing a 'motivating purpose', so long as it is value creating in itself.

Business success, not personal contribution

Most managers, other than CEOs, are judged against some personal contribution which is perceived by others and which determines the fate of their careers. In one organization, playing it safe but always delivering the numbers is the key to success. In another, the key may be being prepared to take risks and drive major change. For the CEO, once the honeymoon is over – and it is always over remarkably quickly – getting the business to deliver is all that counts.

Figure 2 illustrates the life cycle of the CEO. It takes time for the CEO's actions to filter through into business performance. In the early days, therefore, personal impact is most important. In the first three months the CEO is expected to demonstrate an understanding of the business and to start building a strong team. By the end of six months the CEO should have presented a new strategy. By this stage, business performance is beginning to be important, but the CEO can still expect to be judged against the credibility of the new strategy. After the first year, however, there should be clear signs of improvement in business performance; and by the end of year two, there must be a significant upturn.

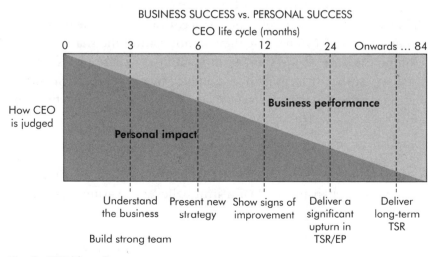

Fig. 2 CEO life cycle.
Source: PA analysis.

By the end of year two, the previous track record or charisma of the CEO is far less important than an ability to demonstrate that the business is moving forwards. For the remainder of the tenure, this will remain the case.

As we have seen, then, the importance of the personal impact of the CEO soon gives way to their ability to drive forward business performance. The question is: what do we mean by business performance?

Business performance defined

For the owners of the business, the answer is simple: they have invested money in buying the shares of the company and they want a return. Specifically, the return they require is what is normally referred to as total shareholder return (TSR): this is a combination of the capital growth in the value of the share and the dividend yield. Ultimately, it is the TSR by which any chief executive of a quoted company will be judged. *No managers who have delivered a poor long-term TSR have ever been regarded as good CEOs.*

Given this fact, it might be expected that all CEOs would possess a good understanding of this measure by which they are judged, and the ways in which they can best sustain a high long-term TSR. In fact, very few do so. According to our research, *only 26 per cent*[1] of CEOs have set themselves a target for long-term TSR. There are two main reasons for this. Unlike internal measures of performance, CEOs have little or no day-to-day control of TSR because they do not control the share price. In addition, because of the short-term volatility of share prices, TSR is not a very revealing measure over a one- or two-year period. So, many managers retreat to the safe haven of an internal measure that they can control directly, such as earnings per share.

Using such measures can, however, prove misleading over the long term. During the 1990s, a leading UK-based industrial conglomerate was run by a charismatic CEO. A firm believer in earnings per share

---

[1] Question 27 – 26 per cent Strongly Agree/Agree with statement 'We derive strategic goals by cascading from an explicit TSR Target', *2002 Survey on Managing for Shareholder Value*, PA Consulting Group.

(EPS), the CEO ran the business exclusively with the aim of driving up reported EPS year on year. In this regard he was very successful. EPS rose steadily throughout the 1990s, largely by means of a targeted acquisition strategy. Nevertheless, at the end of the decade the share price was still very close to where it started in 1990. The company had underperformed dramatically.

The CEO was convinced that the lack of growth in the share price was because the stock markets were unable to appreciate his accomplishments in producing a large, fast-growing and highly profitable business. Analysis of the business performance in a little more detail, however, showed that almost all the growth in the business had been acquisitive growth – there had been almost no net organic growth over this period; and that although earnings per share had been rising, the company was systematically overpaying for these acquisitions, given the growth potential of the acquired businesses. Consequently, it was, on average, *destroying shareholder value*.

By the end of the decade, the CEO was gone, forced out by activist shareholders. A talented CEO with the ability to drive a large organization to deliver extraordinary results over a sustained period of time, he had just one problem: they were the wrong results.

This example highlights the dangers facing a CEO who drives the business in a direction inconsistent with the creation of long-term shareholder value.

The challenge, then, is twofold: to understand total shareholder return and what drives it; and to understand how this relates to the other goals that the organization may have.

Seventeen years of total shareholder return (TSR) growth at Lloyds TSB

Over 17 years, until December 2000, Lloyds Bank shareholders saw the value of their investment, with dividends reinvested, increase over 65 times, doubling and redoubling total shareholder return every 35 months. This was the record of Sir Brian Pitman during his tenure at the top of the Group, first as Chief Executive for 13 years and then as Chairman for four years.

Sir Brian's success came from his unrelenting focus on shareholder value. He argues that a single governing objective enables people at all levels to align their efforts. In Lloyds' case, 'time needed to double the value of the company' was used as the metric of success. Sir Brian believes that generating consistently superior shareholder returns is the best long-term measure of a company's performance and health, as well as an important driver of society's overall economic health.

Sir Brian succeeded in embedding this philosophy throughout the organization by insisting that remuneration be dependent on achieving ambitious, value-based growth targets. Underpinning the deep cultural changes that ensued was a highly effective system of compensation, consisting of appropriate reward systems and stock ownership plans that aligned the interests of employees and shareholders. In large measure, it was Sir Brian's ability to align actions and objectives that resulted in the bank producing such outstanding results for shareholders. He states:

> For people to be truly committed to a strategy of shareholder value creation, they have to believe in it. They have to believe, for example, that economic profit is more important than growth in size, which, pursued for its own sake, usually destroys value. They have to believe in the importance of focusing on those businesses with profitable growth potential and getting rid of those companies, and parts of companies, that cannot earn a return above the cost of capital. Sustainable and profitable growth comes from giving customers new reasons to buy and keep buying. You have to find new ways to be distinctive and to have the courage to invest in it. Above all, CEOs must resist the propensity to grow regardless of the consequences to shareholders – an extremely tenacious force that works incessantly against achieving shareholder returns. If they adopt such convictions – and don't simply pay lip service to them – it will change the way they run their businesses.

Sir Brian's actions as CEO, and later as Chairman, followed this logic unerringly. Besides incentivizing managers to act like owners, he ensured that Lloyds TSB competed only in markets where it could create value. Armed with a thorough understanding of both market dynamics and Lloyds' competitive advantage, he exited potentially value-destroying markets, such as investment banking, and increasingly focused on growing customer value, investing in differentiation and in markets with positive and high returns most likely to create value.

Sir Brian's drive and commitment enabled him to shape the beliefs and actions of his people – and hence to drive corporate performance. Ultimately, it was Sir Brian's passion for value that enabled him to double the value of the bank every three years for 17 years – a level of achievement on a par with market stars such as General Electric and Gillette.

Setting the target

Total shareholder return is a very challenging measure to be judged by: it has a ratchet effect – to sustain a good TSR, however well you do, you need to do better in the future. In crude terms, a TSR target can be taken as roughly equivalent to a target to double the value of the business.

As Figure 3 shows, setting an appropriate TSR target is not that straightforward.

The minimum acceptable TSR is around ten per cent. This corresponds

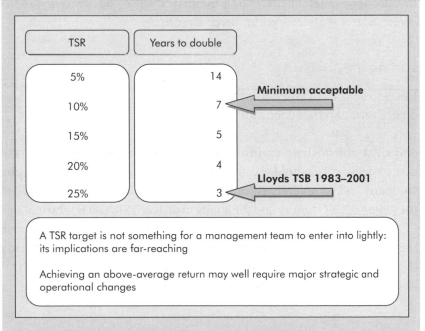

TSR	Years to double
5%	14
10%	7 — Minimum acceptable
15%	5
20%	4
25%	3 — Lloyds TSB 1983–2001

A TSR target is not something for a management team to enter into lightly: its implications are far-reaching

Achieving an above-average return may well require major strategic and operational changes

Fig. 3 Setting a TSR target.
Source: PA analysis.

to the shareholder's cost of equity (the minimum return which will compensate them for the risk of holding shares) and is roughly equivalent to doubling the value of the business every seven years. This, however, is the *absolute minimum*.

To be seen as a good performer, a CEO must deliver more than this. A creditable performance would be 15 per cent, which gives the CEO five years to double the value. A 20 per cent target equates to four years, and few companies can achieve this.

Fewer still can manage a 25 per cent TSR, which gives managers only three years to double the value of the business. Sustaining this level of performance over a long period is extremely difficult and represents world-class shareholder value creation. While Sir Brian Pitman was Chief Executive of Lloyds Bank in the UK, the firm averaged 25 per cent per annum TSR. A remarkable performance.

Whatever else you achieve, you must get the business to deliver shareholder value

In our view, whatever else the CEO may want to do, *delivering shareholder value* is mandatory – for three reasons.

Lasting the course

CEO job tenure, and therefore the freedom to pursue other aims, depends on delivering shareholder value.

Any CEO who wishes to control the destiny of a company must first take care to deliver shareholder value. Otherwise any ability to influence the company will be severely curtailed. There is a stark correlation between the length of CEO tenure and the ability to deliver TSR. CEOs who manage to deliver above-average annualized TSR, in the 20 per cent and above range, are likely to have nine-plus years in which to shape the company they run. Turn in a five per cent or less annualized TSR, and the CEO is likely to have left the company before six years are up.[2]

---

[2] PA analysis.

Long-term health of the business

If the CEO does not create shareholder value, then the business cannot continue to grow or to invest in developing new products or providing high levels of customer service. The dynamics (in a simplified form) are illustrated in Figure 4. This picture illustrates that no business can be healthy if it is not generating shareholder value.

Starting at the left, a business must be able to invest in new products and markets to remain healthy; otherwise its products will become undifferentiated and unattractive to customers. Ultimately, that will harm both its margins and its growth potential. Conversely, differentiated products, for which customers are prepared to pay, provide a basis both for earning an attractive return on investment and for growing the business.

An attractive return on investment is a fundamental prerequisite for shareholder value creation: unattractive investments do not create shareholder value.

Growth is more complex. Growing a business that generates a good return on investment is the best way of creating shareholder value. Growing a

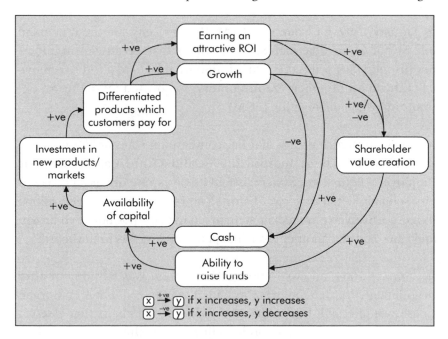

Fig. 4 Long-term impact of value creation and destruction
Source: PA analysis.

business with unattractive returns, however, simply expands the scale of the problem and destroys shareholder value ever more quickly. This distinction between good and bad growth is critical to business success.

Even good growth has one negative side effect: it consumes cash. In fact, any business whose growth rate is higher than its post-tax return on equity will be a net consumer of cash during its growth period. So, even though the growth is good, external funding will be required. A business that consumes cash may still have sufficient capital, as long as it has the ability to raise funds. But this ability will dry up very rapidly if shareholder value is not being created.

Without availability of capital, the business will be unable to invest in new products and markets and, as stated before, its health is therefore gravely endangered.

Shareholder activism

Shareholders are becoming increasingly forceful in ensuring that they get a fair return. If they feel that they are not, then they will intervene even to the point of taking control of a company.

In January 1999, for example, PDFM, Hermes Lens and the Prudential told Mirror Group Chairman Sir Victor Blank that, because of an underperforming share price, they would support any board effort to remove CEO David Montgomery. Montgomery was ousted following an extraordinary general meeting (EGM).

Xerox is another company that has come under shareholder pressure to take specific actions. In April 2003, CalPERS, the California Public Employees' Retirement System, issued its Corporate Governance Focus List, sending a letter to Xerox Chairman and CEO Anne Mulcahy, asking the company to take immediate steps to separate the position of chairman and CEO, and add another three independent directors to the board.

In January 2004, an environmental resolution was withdrawn after negotiation with shareholders. Instead, it was agreed that J. P. Morgan Chase would establish an office of environmental affairs that assesses the environmental impact of projects financed by the firm.

The trend towards active shareholders has been increasing over recent decades, driven partly by the emergence of tracker funds that hold shares in all companies in an index. If a tracker fund is dissatisfied with the performance of a company then, unlike an active fund, it cannot simply sell the stock. It has only two options: ignore the problem or use its power to change the company direction, or even the composition of the board. This trend towards increasing activism is unlikely to reverse.

Creating long-term shareholder value entails making an economic profit

Creating long-term shareholder value means that CEOs need to understand the fundamental economics of their business. Above all, they need to measure profits realistically as economic profit: profit after tax, less a charge for the equity tied up in the business. After all, they cannot create new value for shareholders if they are not even paying them back for the capital they have already lent to the business.

In a 1995 *Harvard Business Review* article, Peter Drucker, probably the greatest management guru of the twentieth century, said:

> What we call profits, the money left to service equity, is usually not profit at all. Until a business returns a profit that is greater than its cost of capital, it operates at a loss. Never mind that it pays taxes as if it had a genuine profit. The enterprise still returns less to the economy than it devours in resources … Until then it does not create wealth; it destroys it.

Long-term shareholder value can be accelerated by pursuing a 'motivating purpose'

The arguments outlined above show that there is an unanswerable case for CEOs to ensure that their businesses maximize long-term shareholder value. When they come to work in the mornings, however, few people are motivated solely by the need to create long-term shareholder value. Most people intuitively feel that it is important to be creating value for other stakeholders, in particular for customers. Many people believe, despite the evidence to the contrary, that creating value for customers is a *sufficient* goal in itself and will ensure the health of the business. Though this is not true, it is actually close to the truth. Creating value for customers is not sufficient to ensure the health of the business, but it is *necessary*.

In Figure 5, the stakeholder picture of a company, the company in the centre survives by transacting directly with a series of stakeholder groups. Each group receives value in some form from the company, but also provides value to the company. Customers, for example, receive products and services and provide cash; employees receive cash and provide effort and ideas; suppliers receive cash in return for products and services; and investors receive cash at a time when a company needs it less (hopefully), in return for providing cash at a time when a company needs it more.

All of these stakeholders have some power to penalize the company if they are not getting value from their transaction: they each have the power to withdraw from their transaction altogether. Customers, for example, will not buy products and services if they feel they do not represent value for money. Self-evidently, the business is sustainable only if it can sustain transactions with each of its stakeholder groups, and, therefore, only so long as it continues to provide value to each of these groups. A good business is one that can create value for all stake-

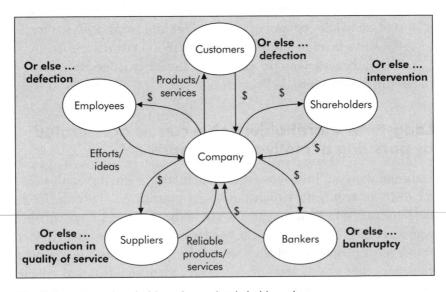

Fig. 5 Long-term shareholder value and stakeholder value.
Source: PA analysis.

holder groups and capture enough of that value to be able to share it with the other stakeholder groups. This is very challenging to do, and requires a great deal of commitment from a large number of people within the organization. That commitment is, in itself, valuable and brings us to the concept of a motivating purpose.

There are three criteria for a motivating purpose for a business:

- It must make *economic sense* to do it, i.e. it must create shareholder value

- It must be *feasible* to do it

- It must be something that large numbers of people within the organization are *prepared to commit to doing* – or it will not happen.

These criteria illustrate both the value of a good mission statement for an organization and the practical difficulty in creating it. The value is that it helps to produce commitment from a large enough body within the organization to ensure delivery. The practical difficulty lies in defining a motivating set of stakeholder goals that are consistent with maximizing shareholder value. This issue is dealt with more fully later in the book (Part 2, Section 7: An organization that knows itself).

In summary

Despite the many possible purposes for a business, the overriding purpose must be, if there is to be a successful business at least, to sustain long-term creation of shareholder value:

- The CEO must move beyond his or her personal contribution and get the business to deliver shareholder value.

- In its most basic terms this means making an economic profit: a profit that rewards shareholders adequately for investing their capital and one that provides an adequate total shareholder return.

- There may be room for, and value in, pursuit of a so-called 'motivating purpose', but only one that fits in with the value-creation purpose of the business – i.e. it creates value, rather than destroying it.

These are some basic CEO ground rules. Sticking to these ground rules is not easy. It involves a number of challenges for the CEO, namely:

- To understand long-term shareholder value

- To understand what it takes to create it

- To work out what needs to happen for *your organization* to become a high-performing organization.

2 Who is the complete CEO?

'We would like you to be our new CEO,' the chairman says. 'We'd like you to run the business. We're here to support you if you need us, but it's up to you how you do it.' And so starts day one as the new leader.

CEOs are invested with great authority and responsibility. Expectations are high and the challenges are difficult. At the same time, if they focus their efforts in the right places, they can lead their organization to a great future, and deliver exceptional performance.

If the purpose of the CEO is obvious – the creation of long-term shareholder value – in practice the role of the CEO is far less clearly defined. Functional roles have specific tasks, textbook and regulatory. The finance director's role is very clear. The marketing director's role is essentially defined by the activities of the function. The CEO's role covers all of these areas, but non-specifically. Should the CEO behave like a generalist who gets involved in everything, a high-level project manager who oversees timescales and delivery, or is there something specific the CEO needs to do which nobody else does?

There are many successful CEOs. Some of them are well known, such as Lord Browne of oil giant BP and Meg Whitman of online auction eBay, while others are much less known than the companies they lead, such as William Weldon of Johnson & Johnson or Alan Latley of Procter & Gamble.

There is no obvious common factor behind their success. Warren Buffett is the scientifically minded capital allocator of Berkshire Hathaway, while Steve Jobs is the creative visionary of design-led Apple. Steve Ballmer is the solid operational boss of Microsoft, providing a counterpoint to the technical genius of his own boss, Chairman and Chief Software Architect, Bill Gates.

Who is the complete CEO?

Given the diversity of leaders and the challenges they face, it would be foolish to single out one person as the perfect CEO role model. Instead, it is better to look at a number of high-performing CEOs; to look at what they do, and what we can learn from them.

If total shareholder return (TSR) is the measure by which the success of CEOs is ultimately judged, who better to study than those CEOs, and the firms that they lead, that have consistently produced a better than average TSR. We focused on a number of companies selected from the world's 100 best-performing large companies (market capitalization greater than £10 billion) based on long-term TSR (see Figure 6).

We might have hoped to find a simple answer to the question of what CEOs have to do to be successful. Perhaps there would be a common style of behaviour that marks out the winners from the losers; perhaps one particular type of business solution would lead to disproportionate success. Unfortunately, we found the opposite: no one style for a CEO will always be appropriate; no one set of actions will always work. Indeed, no CEO born has *all* the skills that would be needed to be the complete CEO. The challenge, therefore, for new CEOs is to find what will work in the context of their own personality and skills, and of the challenges faced by the business they are running.

From Figure 6, we have selected ten companies and their CEOs for more detailed analysis: direct computer company Dell; consumer electronics firm Best Buy; the Royal Bank of Scotland; Lowe's, a DIY home improvement retailer with 850 stores in the USA; HSBC; retailer Tesco; Microsoft; Samsung; Nokia; and Starbucks. (You will find case studies of the CEOs in charge of these companies interspersed throughout the book.)

Name	Country	Industry Sector	Annualized TSR	Market Cap ($bn)
Dell Inc	US	Technology	52%	$80
Gilead Sciences Inc	US	Pharmaceutical	40%	$19
Qualcomm Inc	US	Communications	40%	$62
Cia De Bebidas Das Americas	Brazil	Brewing	39%	$19
Petrobras - Petroleo Bras	Brazil	Energy	37%	$62
Time Warner Inc	US	Communications	36%	$80
SLM Corp	US	Financial	35%	$20
Guidant Corp	US	Medical Instruments & Supplies	34%	$22
Starbucks Corp	US	Retail	34%	$18
Capital One Financial Corp	US	Financial	32%	$20
Hang Seng Bank Ltd	Hong Kong	Financial	30%	$25
Countrywide Financial Corp	US	Financial	29%	$20
Lehman Brothers Holdings Inc	US	Financial	29%	$28
Great-West Lifeco Inc	Canada	Financial	28%	$21
Suncor Energy Inc	Canada	Energy	28%	$26
Suntrust Banks Inc	US	Financial	28%	$24
Power Financial Corp	Canada	Financial	28%	$19
Best Buy Co Inc	US	Retail	28%	$22
Citigroup Inc	US	Financial	27%	$217
Golden West Financial Corp	US	Financial	27%	$18
Banco Bradesco S.A.	Brazil	Financial	27%	$19
Endesa S.A.	Spain	Utilities	27%	$23
Stryker Corp	US	Medical Instruments & Supplies	27%	$21
Automatic Data Processing	US	Technology	27%	$23

Fig. 6 The world's 100 high-performance companies. The table shows the world's 100 top-performing companies in terms of annualized total shareholder return over a ten-year period (1994–2004). To qualify, companies had to have a market capitalization of at least £10 billion on 1st January, 2005. (Continued on following pages.)

Source: PA analysis.

Name	Country	Industry Sector	Annualized TSR	Market Cap ($bn)
Cia Vale Do Rio Doce	Brazil	Basic Materials	27%	$38
MBNA Corp	US	Financial	27%	$30
US Bancorp	US	Financial	26%	$52
Cisco Systems Inc	US	Communications	26%	$108
Target Corp	US	Retail	26%	$45
Telefonos De Mexico SA de CV	Mexico	Communications	25%	$21
Australia and New Zealand Banking Group Ltd	Australia	Financial	24%	$30
Amgen Inc	US	Medical Instruments & Supplies	24%	$95
Samsung Electronics Co Ltd	South Korea	Technology	24%	$76
Boston Scientific Corp	US	Medical Instruments & Supplies	23%	$21
Aflac Inc	US	Financial	23%	$21
SAP AG	Germany	Technology	23%	$52
Microsoft Corp	US	Technology	23%	$278
Banco Bilbao Vizcaya Argenta	Spain	Financial	23%	$55
Commonwealth Bank Of Australia	Australia	Financial	23%	$35
Canadian Natural Resources	Canada	Energy	23%	$26
Genzyme Corp	US	Biotechnology	23%	$18
Merrill Lynch & Co Inc	US	Financial	23%	$52
United Technologies Corp	US	Industrial	23%	$49
Costco Wholesale Corp	US	Retail	22%	$20
Walgreen Co	US	Retail	22%	$44
Westpac Banking Corporation	Australia	Financial	22%	$27
Morgan Stanley	US	Financial	22%	$53
Medtronic Inc	US	Medical Instruments & Supplies	22%	$66
Progressive Corp	US	Financial	22%	$18
Washington Mutual Inc	US	Financial	22%	$35

Fig. 6 (Continued.)

Name	Country	Industry Sector	Annualized TSR	Market Cap ($bn)
Nokia Oyj	Finland	Communications	22%	$68
Shell Canada Ltd	Canada	Energy	21%	$27
Taiwan Semiconductor Manufacturing Company	Taiwan	Technology	21%	$38
Lowe's Cos Inc	US	Retail	21%	$48
Danske Bank A/S	Denmark	Financial	21%	$19
Sysco Corp	US	Food Wholesale	21%	$20
Freddie Mac	US	Financial	21%	$38
Sanofi-Aventis	France	Pharmaceutical	21%	$115
Wells Fargo & Company	US	Financial	21%	$96
Baxter International Inc.	US	Healthcare	21%	$24
Telefonica S.A	Spain	Communications	21%	$79
Applied Materials Inc	US	Technology	21%	$28
Royal Bank Of Scotland Group	UK	Financial	20%	$91
American Express Co	US	Financial	20%	$66
Oracle Corp	US	Technology	20%	$66
Franklin Resources Inc	US	Financial	20%	$20
Novo Nordisk	Denmark	Pharmaceutical	20%	$18
Tyco International Ltd	Bermuda	Industrial	20%	$54
Unicredito Italiano SpA	Italy	Financial	20%	$36
Toronto-Dominion Bank	Canada	Financial	20%	$32
Allied Irish Banks Plc	Ireland	Financial	20%	$18
Intel Corp	US	Technology	20%	$148
Royal Bank Of Canada	Canada	Financial	20%	$43
Bank Of Montreal	Canada	Financial	19%	$23
Fifth Third Bancorp	US	Financial	19%	$22
Intl Business Machines Corp	US	Technology	19%	$122

Fig. 6 (Continued.)

Name	Country	Industry Sector	Annualized TSR	Market Cap ($bn)
General Dynamics Corp	US	Industrial	19%	$22
BB&T Corporation	US	Financial	19%	$21
Canadian Imperial Bank Of Commerce	Canada	Financial	19%	$19
Bank Of America Corp	US	Financial	19%	$166
Bank Of New York Co Inc	US	Financial	19%	$23
Texas Instruments Inc	US	Technology	19%	$51
EMC Corp/Mass	US	Technology	19%	$30
Iberdrola SA	Spain	Utilities	19%	$23
Nike Inc	US	Retail	18%	$19
HSBC Holdings Plc	UK	Financial	18%	$176
Barclays Plc	UK	Financial	18%	$63
Johnson & Johnson	US	Healthcare	18%	$180
Wal-Mart Stores Inc	US	Retail	18%	$179
Allstate Corp	US	Financial	18%	$35
Sasol Ltd	South Africa	Energy	18%	$23
General Electric Co	US	Industrial	18%	$338
Exelon Corp	US	Utilities	18%	$35
Tesco Plc	UK	Retail	18%	$45
Apache Corp	US	Energy	18%	$22
National Australia Bank Ltd	Australia	Financial	17%	$36
Banco Santander Central Hisp	Spain	Financial	17%	$75
Anheuser-Busch Cos Inc.	US	Brewing	17%	$33
Altria Group Inc	US	Consumer	17%	$139
Muenchener Rueckver Ag-Reg	Germany	Financial	17%	$25

Fig. 6 (Concluded.)

The common link between these companies is that not only have they all delivered sustained high returns to their shareholders, but also they have all explicitly worked towards this as their specific goal. This requires clear direction and objectives, and it also requires business design and delivery that actually achieves and sustains it.

What should a CEO do to create a high-performance company like these? To help understand what it takes to be the complete CEO we need to look at three aspects of the CEO's job:

- **The results by which a CEO is judged**: how to measure success; and how to achieve high performance

- **The role of a CEO today**: what they should and should not do; where their priorities should be; and how they relate to others

- **The realities of being a CEO**: what they should do day by day; how to get started; and how to work towards greatness.

Results of the CEO

One of the most important messages in this book is that – for the CEO at least – personal success is business success. In other roles across the business, discrete tasks can be measured by discrete outputs. However, the only measure of the value added by the CEO is the overall performance of the business.

From the selected high-performance companies we can see some themes in the way they have achieved their status, but also considerable variation:

- *Innovators*: at least half of the top ten companies have reshaped their markets in some way. Consider, for example, the role Starbucks played in redefining the coffee shop market by offering high-quality coffee in a social environment. Dell and Capital One are also excellent examples.

- *Focus*: the majority of the high-performing companies have a very clear focus on what their business does. Lowe's knows that its business is about DIY retailing and nothing else. Best Buy sticks with electronics, recognizing that that is what it is famous for, and does well at.

- *Distinctive*: each appears to understand clearly how it is different. This competitive advantage ranges from product features to targeting niche markets, such as Lowe's targeting female DIY buyers.

- *Transformers*: our high-performers have all experienced at least some, and in many cases very significant, change as they have grown organically and by acquisition. Microsoft's entry into PC gaming through the launch of Xbox is a good example.

Becoming a complete CEO means delivering in all these areas.

Role of the CEO

The 'hero' CEO, such as former GE CEO Jack Welch, was widely perceived as a winning model for CEOs. In some cases this model is appropriate, but it is not the only way, nor, in many cases, is it the best. The nature of companies today is one of collaboration, creativity and complexity. No one person can inject all these disciplines.

Instead of a hero, a charismatic talisman, the new leader should be a pragmatic dreamer, a person with an original but achievable vision. Invariably these dreams are only realizable if there are exceptional people to help make it happen. Consequently, one of the most important roles the leader performs is that of team builder; and recruiting a great team requires an ability to create a vision so compelling and seductive that the very best people want to be part of its success.

The leader must create a style that suits the whole team, adapting traditional models and personal traits to the needs of the business. Indeed, it is often the leadership team that sets the values and culture of the whole organization, and determines how the organization is perceived by customers.

Sir Richard Branson, founder and Chairman of the many-faceted Virgin Group, has a very distinctive style. This swashbuckling, sweater-wearing, laid-back CEO is far removed from the conventional image of a be-suited corporate boss. His sense of fun and laid-back style has permeated throughout the organization he runs, shaping both the internal culture and the external perception.

Today's CEOs must adopt a number of different roles. These include:

- *The Director*. The fall of the celebrity CEO is well documented and reflects a shift in CEO from 'lead actor' to 'film director'. The director CEO gives direction and sits at the apex of a decision-making tree.

- *The Face*. The demand for greater accountability and transparency in organizations means that people want to know who is responsible. The representative CEO steps forward as the public face of the business.

- *The Thinker*. The rise in importance of intangible assets reflects a shift from production to service- and knowledge-based organizations. The thinker CEO is the guardian of intellectual property.

- *The Connector*. The increasing complexity and fragmentation of businesses means that somebody needs to bring the pieces together, see the links, and make the connections. The connector CEO is at the hub of the business.

- *The Investor.* The diversity of projects within a business today means that there are many calls on capital. The investor CEO is the allocator of funds, acting rather like a venture capitalist in making investments and seeking a return.

- *The Coach*. One of the biggest challenges is to create the leaders of the future. Coach CEOs work hard to recruit and build a great team around them, to deliver great performance today, and become great CEOs tomorrow.

- *The Exemplar*. The CEO sets the fundamental standards and values the company is expected to observe. The CEO demands no behaviour from others that he or she is not prepared to observe.

Reality of the CEO

It would be easy if the CEO's job were merely a question of strategic thinking. Decide how performance is to be measured: TSR. Then identify a number of important actions that must be taken in order to deliver that performance.

As any CEO will know, business life is not like this. The CEO's reality is different: a gruelling and complex schedule of meetings and memos, some of them essential, others more a formality.

The CEO's presence is requested at conferences, events, dinners and awards ceremonies. Each day could be spent chairing meetings, and every evening with a black tie and a free meal. No wonder that CEOs guard their schedules jealously.

Then there is the information overload. Everybody wants to let the CEO know what is going on. Witness the mountainous in-tray, the number of emails each morning, particularly the number of emails that 'cc' the CEO. The whole day might be spent just reading emails. But CEOs do not have time to read long reports and proposals. Consequently, allocation of time is a key to effectiveness.

And then there is the perception of the über-CEO. Yet CEOs are not necessarily the best people around – the most intelligent, the most numerate, the most expert. Just as in sports teams, the team captain is often not the star performer. CEOs don't have to be superstars. Just effective CEOs. The CEO's role is a distinct one, just as the CFO or CTO's is. They are not interchangeable. A fantastic finance director will not necessarily create a great CEO, nor vice versa.

Indeed, one of the best tips for a CEO comes from Gates himself, who is happy to explain that one of his secrets in turning Microsoft into a commercial success is to 'surround yourself by people better than you'.

In summary

As we have seen, there is no magic formula for being a successful CEO. There are no silver bullets: no single leadership style for a CEO will always be appropriate; no one set of actions will always prove effective.

Instead, CEOs – aspiring, new or existing – have to discover for themselves what will work within the context of their own personality, skills and the challenges faced by the business they are running.

To help understand what it takes to be the complete CEO, CEOs should consider three things: the results by which a CEO is judged, the role of a CEO today and the realities of being a CEO.

And, while there is no magic formula for becoming the complete CEO, the high-performance model outlined in Part 2 of this book will help provide some answers.

3 Management and leadership

We have seen that there seem to be no simple answers – and in one sense this seems obvious: if there really were a few well-defined things you had to do to be a successful CEO, filling the post would be a trivial matter. On the other hand, we constantly read about leadership skills (which, admittedly, are not well defined) – perhaps what is needed is to be a great leader, and all else will follow. Sadly, even this is not true. What we have found is this:

- Leadership and management are different things

- Strong management is necessary but not sufficient to ensure good performance

- Strong leadership is also necessary but not sufficient to be a great CEO; therefore, you need to understand and combine the two.

Leadership and management are different things

Before discussing the relationship between leadership and management, it is worth noting that the terms are often confused or used interchangeably. In this book, we adopt the following definitions:

- **Management** is about rational decision-making: the output of management is decisions; the output of good management is the right decisions.

- **Leadership** is about creating a collective commitment to delivering high performance: the output of leadership is action; the output of good leadership is strong business results.

Leadership and management are very different activities. However, they are also complementary activities, and both can be performed by the same CEO.

In fact, to be successful, CEOs must consciously combine management and leadership. Without management – the ability to make good decisions – leadership qualities can be positively lethal, as General Custer's soldiers discovered at Little Big Horn. But without leadership, good management founders because good decisions are not executed by subordinates. Napoleon's normally brilliant leadership skills deserted him at Waterloo, a battle during which he grumbled perpetually about the blunders of his generals.

Management is necessary but not sufficient

The output of management is decisions. The output of good management is the right decisions; conversely, of course, bad management results in the wrong decisions – and these can be very costly.

A huge amount of 'corporate vandalism' has been caused in the last few years by significant incorrect decisions. This is most obviously true in the case of 'bet-the-ranch' decisions, many of which ended up losing the ranch, but is equally true of smaller, but nevertheless harmful, decisions.

There are many examples. It is well known that the majority of acquisitions destroy shareholder value, yet year after year the pattern of poor decision-making continues. Many telcos almost destroyed themselves with their decisions to pay over the odds for 3G licences. Most major forays into the 'new economy' were complete failures. Many capital-intensive industries are plagued with chronic overcapacity, because decision-making is not sufficiently aligned with business reality.

Trillions of dollars have been lost and many careers have stalled or failed because of poor decision-making. Good management is *necessary* for business success.

For the CEO, however, good management poses a number of challenges.

First, there are many important decisions taken in any organization that are essential to get right; too many, in fact, for the CEO to become personally involved in all of them. Of these decisions, even some of the most important decisions – those in which the CEO must play a role – may lie outside the CEO's personal areas of competence and comfort.

There are other obstacles that make decision-making, and thus management, a challenging proposition. It is not always easy to get at the facts. This may be because the organization is poor at collecting external data. It may be simply because the data is intrinsically 'fuzzy'. Finally, management is both an analytical and a creative activity. Managers must reflect this balance in capability and behaviour.

Later on in this book we explore how the CEO can address these challenges to improve the quality of decision-making in the organization.

Even when the CEO is a good manager, and manages to get to grips with the decision-making aspect of the role, it is no guarantee of success – even if the decision is the correct one. Decisions on their own are no guarantee of delivery, for three reasons:

- *Capability.* A decision will not deliver if it does not reflect the capabilities of the organization – indeed, it is impractical if it does not do so. These are criteria that should have been part of the initial decision-making process.

- *Commitment.* A decision will not deliver if, once taken, it is then evaluated through yet more analysis to the point of paralysis. Better to say, 'OK, decision made, let's do it.'

- *Engagement.* A decision will not deliver if it does not engage the people who must implement the decision. The understanding and conviction, upon which the decision was made, must be communicated to the people who are to implement that decision. This is one of the most common problems where decision-making is concerned: many brilliant strategy reports gather dust in filing cabinets; many well-meaning initiatives fail to deliver, because they engage only a small proportion of those needed to implement them.

It is clear, therefore, that while good management is necessary, on its own it is not *sufficient* to guarantee good performance.

Leadership is necessary but not sufficient

The output of leadership is action. Leadership is about stimulating the right understanding and emotional commitment in others.

Leaders inspire action, engaging people to drive change. This is why charisma is so often (but incorrectly) cited as an essential attribute of leadership. In fact, as previously outlined, there are many ways for leaders to inspire people and carry followers with them.

Leaders must provide a bridge, to translate decisions into actions. This bridging process is complex. It is partly about providing a confidence booster that the new is possible. This can be done in various ways: taking a management team to see what has been accomplished elsewhere, setting up a pilot to demonstrate on a small scale what can be done, or even simply benchmarking performance within the organization to show that the target levels are already being achieved in places. Most important is that the leader must be personally convinced, or none of these will work.

Leadership also involves giving managers and staff more practical help in making the connections between a new decision and ways of working. It is about helping them to understand the vision and the rationale behind the decision; how the world will be different in practice; what steps are involved in moving to the new world; and their roles and responsibilities in bringing about the new order, and in preserving the old.

One of the most important imperatives of change management is to articulate the difference between old and new explicitly and honestly. People sometimes shy away from this. Instead, they use weasel words designed to appeal to everyone. It is crucial that a decision must be communicated clearly – what it is, what it is not. And in terms of the actions to implement it, equally – what is required, and what is not.

Later in the book we set out some practical steps that a CEO can take to ensure that effective leadership is taking place, and describe the CEO's role in getting the organization to internalize the future vision.

Leadership is clearly of crucial importance to business success. Unfortunately, it is not on its own sufficient to ensure that success.

It is interesting to compare two great leaders – Steve Jobs and Bill Gates. In shareholder value terms, it is clear that, as a CEO, Bill Gates has been more successful, as evidenced by Microsoft's position in the league table of the world's 100 high-performance companies on page 6. This success most likely resulted from superiority in *combining* leadership and management effectively, rather than from better leadership.

Steve Jobs has demonstrated superb leadership. At Apple computers Jobs created a compelling vision, painting a picture of the highly innovative Apple taking on the corporate Goliath Microsoft. Jobs engaged both Apple employees and customers, building one of the most loyal customer bases of any company. Devout customers are fondly referred to as Apple evangelists and are the envy of many companies. Nevertheless, some of the early decisions taken by Apple condemned it to a minority position in the personal computer market. Brilliant leadership is no substitute for strong management: it is a complement to it.

More recently, but still leading from the front, Jobs drove his staff to extraordinary lengths in order to deliver a remarkable set of products, such as the PowerBook and the iPod, which have gained widespread success. Time will tell whether Jobs will one day be judged as a better manager than Gates.

The CEO must consciously combine leadership and management

The complementary roles of leadership and management can be seen as a traditional yin–yang model: management is more closely aligned with 'yang' terms, such as cool, aggregating, conscious and reasoning; and leadership with 'yin' terms, such as imagining, non-linear, holistic and subjective.

Most importantly, yin and yang are not alternatives. Success requires both. It is also worth remembering that one reinforces the other. In education, a person's pursuit of a creative subject, such as music or art, will add to the analytical capability that enables an appreciation of the patterns within science or mathematics, and vice versa.

CEOs need to know when to lead and when to manage. They should also consciously decide *how* to lead and *how* to manage. It is important to understand as an individual where you are strongest and where you are weakest and to work out explicit strategies for dealing with the weaknesses.

The high-performing CEO: Sir George Mathewson and the Royal Bank of Scotland

Sir George Mathewson took over as CEO of the Royal Bank of Scotland in the early 1990s, faced with the challenge of transforming the sluggish bank into a competitive company. At the time of his arrival the bank was making £26 million against a £200 million target and was vulnerable to takeovers, with HSBC and Standard Chartered mooted as making attempts to acquire it.

Underlying such problems was a huge and inefficient branch system upon which Mathewson unleashed a relentless programme, named 'Project Columbus'. In effect, this was a radical restructuring, aimed at slimming down the company, and included a widespread management clean-out, shedding some 3,500 jobs. In addition, Mathewson removed the back office from the branch and centralized it to create more space for retail and open-plan offices. Such actions established Mathewson as a tenacious reformer, capable of delivering the transformations needed to create one of the best performers in the banking sector and hence deliver shareholder value. By 1998, the bank was earning a pre-tax profit of over £1 billion.

Having forced the bank into shape, Mathewson was able to initiate growth-oriented actions, which involved diversification into the insurance market and expansion of the credit-card business. However, closest to his heart, and a fitting finale to his executive career, was the £21 billion takeover of NatWest, a bank that was three times larger than the Edinburgh-based RBS.

Despite the size of the deal, it is the negotiations leading up to the takeover (which saw Mathewson fight a bitter battle with the Bank of Scotland's CEO, Peter Burt) that caused most interest within the business press. Against a reputation for impatience, Mathewson won through his ability to focus on the long-term gains, delaying announcement of an offer and being favoured for his expansionist as well as cost-cutting focus. Mathewson's career exhibits a CEO who led by example and was able to put long-term profitability before short-term losses. The ten-year annualized TSR for the period 1994–2004 was 20 per cent, highlighting the success of Mathewson's strategy.

Making time to lead and manage

Any CEO will tell you that 'this sounds excellent; I just don't have the time to do it all'. Unfortunately this is all too true in most cases. Consequently, if CEOs are to sustain high performance, they must learn to become brilliant managers of time. Time management and the effective allocation of time, across stakeholders, activities and personal life, is perhaps the most important task of any CEO.

All stakeholders are important at times, and they believe that you, as CEO, owe them some of your time. Your first task is to consider who, among the stakeholders, are most important at any particular time, then, recognizing their relative roles, consider which are most important to you and the success of the business. We set out a systematic approach to this problem later in the book.

A typical current allocation of CEO time across stakeholder groups might look something like this:

- 40 per cent management – work with them, connect their ideas

- 30 per cent staff – be a leader, use your status at the right moments

- 20 per cent investors – keep close to them, educate them and communicate (as we shall see later, this allocation of time may not always be productive)

- 10 per cent customers – lead at the right times, for staff and customers.

The second challenge is to understand the split in time between real (management) and symbolic (leadership) actions. Symbolic actions are important, although the less thoughtful CEO could easily brush them off as meaningless gestures. Indeed, effective symbolism is crucial to good leadership. Symbols range from the choices of people with whom you spend your time, representing the business at events or in the media, making a phone call to say 'well done', to spending time eating in the staff restaurant. Jack Welch habitually wrote handwritten notes that he sent to workers at all levels – from part-time staff to senior executives. Some even framed his notes, as a tangible proof of their leader's appreciation.

Up to 40 per cent of a CEO's time is likely to be symbolic. This might not seem to be the best use of time but it matters to others, and can often have a greater impact on results than other uses of time.

The final time analysis useful to the CEO's role is that of deciphering urgency from importance. Urgent issues can easily dominate your daily life, and totally prevent the creation of the future, or other important matters. It is important to allocate significant amounts of top management time to non-urgent important matters that might otherwise forever be neglected. These issues must be those that drive future greatness.

In summary

Ask yourself, do you need to work out how to be a 'leader' or how to be a 'manager'?

CEOs *must* be leaders *and* managers, and they must perform each of these two tasks well. Leaders who inspire the wrong actions will kill the business … and managers who make decisions that are not implemented are wasting their time. The balance between leading and managing will be different for every company and individual. Finding the right balance will depend on your business, and the team you have in place to support you. It will depend on your capabilities, and the priorities you place within your role.

Part 2

The CEO's High-Performance Model

Part 2 is the heart of this book. It introduces and explores in detail the model of the high-performance CEO. Each section presents a number of principles that are proven to work; they illustrate the practical steps taken by the CEO in order to implement these principles and, where possible, they indicate the degree of impact they have on long-term performance:

- Section 1 sets the CEO on the path to creating a great company. Most CEOs do not inherit a high-performance business – in fact around half of them inherit businesses that are actually destroying shareholder value. This section shows that there are no short cuts to greatness for such businesses.

- Section 2 introduces the CEO's high-performance model. This model sets the personal role of the CEO in the context of the performance of the organization. By ensuring each of the five areas in the model – through the agency of management and leadership – are addressed, the CEO can greatly increase the chances of long-term success.

- Section 3 introduces the idea of a winning business model – one that faces economic reality and directs the company towards making an economic profit. This model creates real shareholder value through efficiently creating and capturing value for customers.

- Section 4 shows that in the process of continually renewing the business model, the CEO must identify, develop and preserve those capabilities and resources that are the key building blocks of future winning business models. These are among the few things that should not be sacrificed to improve short-term value delivery.

- Section 5 tackles leadership. It shows that effective leadership depends on concrete actions taken by the leader and gives examples based on interviews with some of the world's most successful CEOs of what actions they took and why.

- Section 6 is about creating strong management. It shows how the CEO can ensure not only that he or she is a sound manager but also that, as far as possible, management decisions throughout the organization will be sound. This section draws heavily on research carried out with around 1,000 of the world's leading quoted companies.

- Section 7 addresses the issue of an organization that knows itself – how to create a link between the goals, values and priorities of the CEO and the decisions and actions of tens of thousands of individuals who determine what the business actually does.

1 Getting your company ready for greatness

On passing through the airport bookstalls, today's managers are confronted by a bewildering array of texts extolling the virtues of radical new strategies. These books are written by gurus who are household names; they are supported by case studies of immensely successful companies such as GE and Toyota; they are enormously compelling. With all this advice, becoming an excellent performer should be easy.

Back in the real world, around 40 per cent of companies are destroying shareholder value: their investment decisions have, on average, returned below their cost of equity.[1] Clearly, their strategies must be wrong. So, what must CEOs do to get the companies they run on the road to becoming high-performance companies, and secure their position as successful CEOs? How can CEOs be sure that the strategies they implement will create shareholder value?

The answer is that they must recognize that the type of value-creating strategy to deploy depends on the current reality of the business. It is dangerous to rely on what is written in the pages of the gurus' guides unless it clearly relates to what is actually happening to, and in, the company concerned. CEOs must understand the economic reality of their own business, because in most cases that economic reality renders most of what is written irrelevant, or even dangerous – a big strategic leap might destroy the company.

[1]PA analysis of Fortune 500 and FTSE 100.

The truth is that, for most companies, to begin with at least, the vision of great success through radical corporate strategy offered by the countless business books on the subject is a mirage. There is no short cut, or magic potion. Few companies leap to greatness. Most take sensible steps:

- Step one: *understand the internal economics of your company* – this will enable you to deposit the baggage your company is carrying, and in itself add significant value.

- Step two: *understand the external economics and strategic realities your businesses face* – this will enable you to focus scarce resources on to those businesses which can create value sustainably, and will release further value.

- Step three: *distil from these businesses the sources of their competitive advantage and find radical ways of extending and exploiting it* – this unlocks huge value, and leads to what is usually regarded as 'great'.

Most CEOs do not fully understand the economics of their own business

Before setting foot on the steps towards creating a great company, the CEO must first get to grips with the basic economics of the business. In PA's international survey, 70 per cent of companies measured profit in the same way that accountants do.[2] Operating profit, profit before tax or occasionally earnings (profit after tax) were the key measures. Unfortunately, these measures do not tell a company whether it is creating or destroying value in a business.

There is a reliable measure that a company can use to determine whether or not it is creating value. In 1890, British economist Alfred Marshall invented the concept of economic profit (EP): profit after tax, less a charge for the equity tied up in the business. The majority of companies do not yet use this measure.

In the following example, two mature businesses have identical performance and prospects except in one respect: Company A is far more capital-

[2] *Managing for Shareholder Value 2003/4 International Survey Report*, PA Consulting Group.

		Company A	Company B
Accounting view	Operating profit	100	100
	Interest	0	0
	Profit before tax	100	100
	Tax	(30)	(30)
	Profit after tax	70	70
Economic view	Capital employed	1000	500
	–Debt	0	0
	–Equity	1000	500
	Equity charge	(100)	(50)
	Economic profit	(30)	20

Fig. 7 A tale of two companies.
Source: PA analysis.

intensive than Company B. For simplicity, it is assumed that the cost of equity for both businesses – the minimum return which investors would find acceptable – is ten per cent (see Figure 7).

From the point of view of conventional accounting, both businesses are equally profitable; but from the point of view of the economics of the business, only Company B is making money. Is it conceivable that accounting profit fails to answer this most basic of questions: *Is the business creating value?* Unfortunately, it is not only conceivable but also true.

Imagine if both Company A and Company B need to replace their assets to continue trading. To simplify the example, let us assume that they will not need replacing again. The cash-flow implications are detailed in Figure 8.

	Company A	Company B
One-off investment of equity	(1000)	(500)
Incremental post-tax cash flows per annum	70	70
Present value of cash flows	700	700
Net present value	(300)	200

Fig. 8 Cash-flow implications of replacing assets.
Source: PA analysis.

From a cash-flow point of view, Company A is not sustainable: keeping it running or growing it will destroy value, even though it makes an accounting profit. The original shareholders will never get back the money they invested to create the business.

Most companies contain a mixture of business like Company A and business like Company B but, without access to the economic profit measure, they cannot distinguish the two.

Companies often know even less at the product level: many companies report only gross profit. One management team we worked with recently ran the business using information systems that told them that all product groups, and the vast majority of individual products in a 30,000-product range, were profitable. Allocating all costs showed that only 9 out of 12 product groups were profitable and 75 per cent of individual products were loss-making. It is not surprising, therefore, that the overall company was destroying shareholder value.

Strategy formulation requires a sound economic understanding at the company level

Two of the most fundamental issues in strategy formulation are *market attractiveness* and *competitive strength*. Neither of these can be understood without the basis of the economic understanding at the company level described previously.

For a market to be attractive strategically, it has to be possible for several players to make money in it. Size and growth do not necessarily make a market attractive, though they often help; only making money counts and, as we have seen, most businesses use measures that do not tell them whether they, their competitors or even their total market is making money.

A business that has a real competitive advantage makes more economic profit over time than its competitors. It may or may not have a higher quality product (BA vs Ryanair), it may or may not have a lower cost base (Proton vs BMW), but it makes more economic profit.

Without an economic underpinning, basing strategy on these concepts, however powerful they are, can be dangerous.

Radical approaches to strategy are likely to fail without the appropriate economic understanding

Any radically successful strategy involves significant growth and investment. By definition, any strategy whose investments do not return above the cost of equity will fail.

As we have discussed, a strategy that is not based on a sound economic understanding, both internal and external, runs a high risk of returning less than its cost of equity. Therefore, any radical strategy that is not based on a sound economic understanding runs the risk of being a dramatic failure.

Since most companies do not have this solidity of economic understanding, much of the more radical strategy thinking is not just irrelevant for them, it is actually dangerous.

What, then, *should* these companies do to create more value?

The three steps

Step one: understanding and dealing with internal and external economic reality is a valuable first step towards sound performance

A huge performance benefit can be derived from creating and exploiting a robust understanding of internal economics. Three factors are important here:

- Most businesses carry a lot of heavy baggage which inhibits their performance

- Depositing the baggage adds a great deal of value

- Institutionalizing this thinking sustains value creation.

Most businesses carry heavy baggage

PA's experience working with clients suggests that over 40 per cent of capital is often tied up in value-destroying businesses. As stated above, however, only around 30 per cent of businesses measure economic profit (EP).

This means that a significant number of companies are engaged in business activities that are destroying value and the majority are not aware of the fact, because they do not employ the necessary metrics. Figure 9 shows a typical example.

In this case it is clear that the bank is carrying a lot of excess baggage: it is investing heavily in building its investment banking businesses – and most of these investments are destroying shareholder value.

Depositing the baggage adds a great deal of value

The good news about a situation like this is that there are some relatively easy wins: just deposit the baggage. The example of Nokia (see page 70) shows how powerful this can be.

In a situation such as Figure 9, a business that manages on earnings or on operating profit will typically seek to grow all the business units. For the sake of argument, we assume a growth target of ten per cent. If successful, the net result will be a business in which all the numbers are ten per cent higher. No doubt this would be considered a good result.

However, if the business manages by EP then it should focus on growing the value-creating businesses, and at the same time cutting back – where possible – the value-destroying businesses. The net effect will be a dramatically better result.

Our research shows that this is not just a theoretical possibility – it is a measurable, delivered reality: those companies which explicitly linked their strategy to shareholder value delivered on average 11 per cent TSR per annum more than those which did not.[3]

It is important to note that there are certain situations where it may be inappropriate to ditch value-destroying businesses, at least in the short

[3] Source: *Managing for Shareholder Value 2002 International Survey Report,* PA Consulting Group

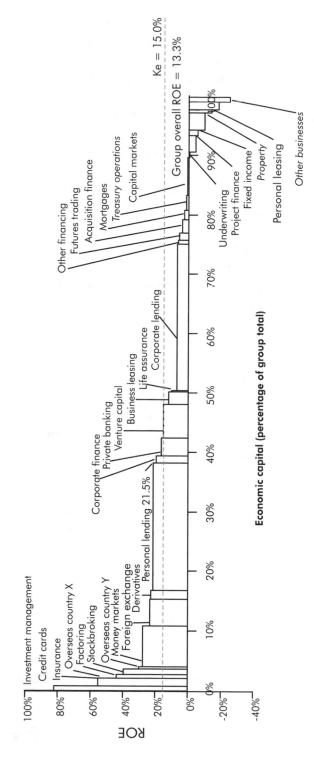

Fig. 9 Value creation in a large European bank.

Source: PA analysis.

term. The three main situations are when the snapshot provided by the economic picture fails to capture the future value-creation potential of a business (e.g. a new venture, or a highly cyclical business at the bottom of its cycle); the unprofitable business is key to supporting a profitable one, and the combined performance is value creating; and the cost of exiting a business would be greater than the cost of keeping it going.

Of course it is usually easy to make a plausible claim that one or more of these is true, and to use this as an argument against action. CEOs must watch out for this, or they will become paralyzed and unable to deposit any baggage at all.

Institutionalizing this thinking sustains value creation

The benefits of focusing on value creation within the business are not a one-off: they are repeatable both over time and at different levels. The arguments that apply to whole businesses apply equally to product groups and individual products, to market segments and even to individual customers.

A business that makes EP the key measurement by which it manages will automatically take decisions in the way suggested above: in allocating capital to Strategic Business Units (SBUs); in planning its future product portfolio and in targeting its market/customer strategies. This will provide benefits for several years as the baggage is gradually deposited.

In the end, however, the business will have left behind all the baggage it can. It will have to do more to create further value. Where should it go next?

Step two: understanding and dealing with external reality is the key to shifting resources into strategically defensible businesses

The next step is to ensure that the business's understanding of the external world is as firmly grounded in economic reality as its measurement of internal economic performance.

Two simple definitions can help to ensure this grounding:

- *Market attractiveness* is defined in this way: an attractive market is one in which the average firm makes an economic profit; specifically, the ratio of the returns of the average company to the cost of equity is above one. On average, players in this market create shareholder value, though not all may do so.

- *Competitive strength* is defined as being able to make more money from your invested capital than your competitors, specifically the ratio of the returns of the company in question (adjusted to stabilize market share if necessary: a business earning two per cent higher returns but losing market share to its competitors may not have any advantage at all) to those of its competitors. If this ratio is above one, the business has a competitive advantage; if below one, it is disadvantaged.

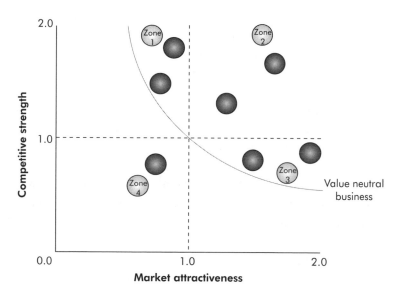

Fig. 10 Market attractiveness and competitive strength.
Source: PA analysis.

[3] Market Attractiveness × Competitive Strength

$$= \frac{\text{average returns}}{\text{cost of equity (Ke)}} \times \frac{\text{company returns}}{\text{average returns}}$$

$$= \frac{\text{company returns}}{\text{Ke}}$$

Figure 10 captures this dynamic.

The product of these two factors *defines* the ability of the business to create value[3]: using these definitions, any strong business in an attractive market will create shareholder value. This is, of course, not necessarily true if size and growth are used to define attractiveness and market share to define advantage.

A business that has fully grasped its internal economics and acted accordingly is unlikely to have many business units below or to the left of the value-neutral line shown in Figure 10. It may still, however, have several business units in Zones 1 and 3. These businesses need rapid attention because both market attractiveness and competitive strength tend to weaken over time unless concrete action is taken.

A business in Zone 1 is in an unattractive market, but makes money because of its competitive strength. Even in the most unattractive markets one player will make money – or in the end the market disappears entirely. Being the last man standing can be a very profitable strategy, but being the last one to fall is most unappealing. The challenge, therefore, is to determine how long the business can remain in Zone 1 – unless the answer is 'for ever', there is a strategic job to be done.

A business in Zone 3 is competitively disadvantaged but makes money because of the enormously attractive market in which it plays. The risk here is that, unless there are extraordinary barriers to entry, new players will be attracted in and returns in the market will be reduced for all players. The disadvantaged players will end up losing money. Again the question is, 'how long can we stay in Zone 3?' Unless the answer is 'for ever', there is a problem.

Thinking this way helps companies to migrate their businesses into sustainable value-creating positions. This can be done in three ways:

• Changing the composition of the portfolio by merger, acquisition and divestment.

• Strengthening the attractiveness of the markets in which Zone 1 businesses play by driving industry restructuring. This is often, but not always, possible.

- Strengthening the competitive position of Zone 3 businesses by applying an understanding of internal, competitive and customer economics (usually possible).

The last point above deserves further elaboration: how can companies go about strengthening their competitive position? The answer depends on understanding two things.

First, there are the customer economics: what is the proposition worth to customers? This requires an analysis of the value provided to the customer. Look at the different aspects of the business – service, lead time, etc. What is their relative value to the customer? How do they rate in terms of the strengths and weaknesses of the business? What weaknesses are important or unimportant? Where is there over-delivery?

Second, there are the internal economics: what do different aspects of the business – service, lead time, etc. – cost to provide in relation to competitors?

By focusing the business on what it can do to create value for its customers, at little extra cost, it is possible to refocus efforts on to value creation and to push a business firmly into Zone 3.

Enormous value can be created by applying this thinking, but eventually companies exhaust the opportunities created: there is no more baggage that can be jettisoned; all the key businesses are well placed in attractive markets; there is little scope for growing returns without sacrificing share or growing share without sacrificing returns.

Where can such a company turn next for its future value growth?

Step three: exploiting unique strengths to fuel growth

By this stage, the CEO has fully understood the business's internal and external economics; understood the drivers of these economics; re-shaped the business accordingly to create a highly profitable, strategically defensible business.

In doing so, the CEO will have created a strategically secure platform, and generated a great deal of shareholder value in the process.

Company	Source of competitive strength
Coca-Cola	A large market share means that Coca-Cola's unit cost of advertising is lower than its competitors'; therefore, its brand will always be stronger which, in this market, means Coca-Cola will always make more money
Microsoft	Microsoft's dominance in operating systems means that it can exert enormous leverage in related business areas
Dell	The unique business system at Dell gives such a cost/service advantage that none of its competitors can respond to it effectively

Fig. 11 Specific sources of competitive advantage.
Source: PA analysis.

Now is the time to create a radical growth strategy. This is the time where the gurus become truly relevant.

Validate the source and applicability of competitive strength

First ensure that the source and applicability of the company's competitive strength are made explicit and validated. This requires a more specific understanding of the source of this advantage, as illustrated in Figure 11 for three well-known corporations. These insights must be fully validated against internal, customer and competitor economics. Once validated, they become extremely powerful.

Exploiting this strength to fuel value growth

Shareholder value is determined as much by growth as by returns. Indeed, in the long run, once returns have peaked (often at around twice the cost of equity in a high-performing business), further value creation depends entirely on growth. In the cases above, the value-creating direction of growth is determined by the sources of competitive advantage:

Exploitation of the brand is key with Coca-Cola. Former CEO Roberto Goizueta understood this and therefore targeted water as the enemy: only when Coca-Cola had substituted for drinking water would the growth potential be exhausted.

At Microsoft, leverage is the opportunity: to move to related areas of software, where compatibility with MS-DOS, and later Windows, is key. This has enabled Microsoft to extend its dominance into office applications and Web browsers, and to threaten the PDA and server markets.

For Dell, there is mileage both in taking further share in its existing markets and in applying similar business design to related markets.

In each of these cases, once the source of competitive advantage has been made explicit – usually easy when it is large – the value-creating direction of growth becomes obvious.

The high-performing CEO: Kun-Hee Lee and Samsung Electronics

In reforming Samsung Electronics from making non-branded appliances for the likes of GE and RCA to challenging Sony as the premier consumer electronics brand, Kun-Hee Lee has turned this star of the giant Korean chaebol, Samsung, into one of Asia's greatest success stories.

Kun-Hee Lee took over control of Samsung Electronics in 1987 and has successfully steered the conglomerate through several significant transformations during his tenure. The largest of these was started in 1993, with Lee stating that, despite appearances to the contrary, Samsung Electronics was suffering from 'terminal cancer'. The cancer Lee recognized was the growing capability of China and the realization that in the longer term Samsung Electronics could not sustain its cost advantage at the lower end of the market.

Lee's response to this challenge was to instruct the managers across his businesses to 'change everything except for your wives and children', and to kick-start a focus on design and innovation, using ideas and best practice from American and European design companies. This was a £126 million programme that involved design and marketing courses for the companies' senior management which, coupled with sustained investment in R&D that accounted for $2.9 billion (8 per cent of revenue) in 2003, Lee believes has delivered Samsung impressive successes, reflected in a ten-year TSR of 24 per cent per annum and profits in 2005 of over $10 billion. Lee also decentralized the business, pushing control and ownership of individual business units down to his managers, enabling them to capitalize quickly on niche opportunities such as LCD screens, which has emerged into a $5 billion business.

Lee is a figurehead CEO, more so than even Gates at Microsoft or Welch at GE, being the second-generation CEO and principal owner of what still remains his family's company. At one stage, following the 1997 Asian economic crisis, Lee even offered $2 billion of his own $4.3 billion fortune to satisfy Samsung's creditors. Lee uses this position, and his position in the wider community – he is a member of the International Olympic

Committee – to create an aura of achievement and charisma that is important to the organization as a whole. Lee is, for example, proud that Samsung attracts the best minds in Korea, and is now looking to develop his management team with the best talent from the global marketplace.

Overall, Lee's legacy will have been in moving Samsung Electronics up-market, taking and adapting Western ideas in design, management and, most recently, in investor relations – the company is eyeing a NYSE listing, making Samsung Electronics a major force in the global marketplace.

In summary

For a business which has created a strategically defensible position, which has articulated and validated its source of competitive strength and which understands the limits of its applicability, the radical options open up.

A business such as this has enormous financial strength; real competitive advantage, whose sources and applicability it understands; and the understanding required to respond to changes in its environment. With this kind of foundation a company has a real chance of using a radical strategy as a route to success.

Companies like Coca-Cola, Microsoft or Dell have spent at least a decade (and in Coca-Cola's case over a century) understanding their business and refining their corporate strategy. For CEOs that want to lead their companies to success there is a simple lesson here. Becoming a successful CEO is bound up with creating a high-performing company – and it takes time. It is a step-by-step process. And, as outlined, the three main steps are:

- Step one: understand the internal economics of your company. This enables you to jettison any excess baggage your company is carrying and, in doing so, add significant value to the business.

- Step two: understand the external economics and strategic realities your company faces. This will enable you to focus scarce resources on those parts of the business that can create value sustainably and, in doing so, release further value.

- Step three: finally, distil from the various parts of the company, from the different business units, the source of competitive advantage. Then find radical ways of extending and exploiting it. This will unlock huge value, and will create what is usually regarded as 'great'.

2 The CEO's high-performance model

Success for the CEO is the creation of long-term shareholder value. However, creating long-term shareholder value is easier said than done. Only around half of all businesses – and therefore only around half of all CEOs – do create value. This raises the question: *What does a CEO need to do in order to create long-term shareholder value successfully?*

Of course, there is no single thing that creates success – there is a long list of factors, and the CEO is ultimately responsible for everything on that list. A key objective of this book is to corral those responsibilities into a single taxonomy that CEOs can use to assess themselves and their organizations.

The high-performance model (see Figure 12) is a taxonomy in the form of a five-pillared model. The five elements are as follows:

- The first step in creating long-term shareholder value comes from building and sustaining a **winning business model**

- A winning business model requires the appropriate building blocks: the **right capabilities and resources**.

- The CEO cannot change a business single-handedly. Building a strong business model and nurturing the right capabilities and resources requires:

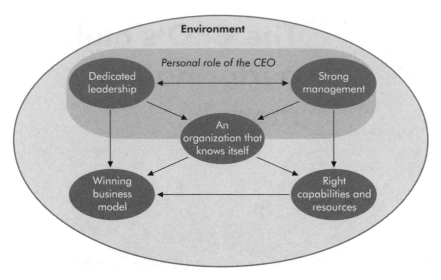

Fig. 12 The high-performance model.
Source: PA analysis.

> **Strong management** – to ensure that the right decisions are made.
> **Dedicated leadership** – to ensure that those decisions translate into action.

- Exceptional performance demands exceptional commitment. The best businesses can be described as **organizations that know themselves** – all members of staff understand what is important, where the company is trying to go and what their personal role is in getting it there – without this, they will inadvertently subvert the business model and weaken the capabilities and resources on which the future of the business depends.

All of these five elements are conditioned by the nature of the business environment, which the CEO must understand and interpret for the organization.

Long-term shareholder value comes from building and sustaining a winning business model

A winning business model creates more value for shareholders. It creates value for customers and captures it more efficiently than the firm's competitors do. It is a business model where the source of competitive advantage is deliberate and well understood; reflected in every aspect of the business from recruitment strategy to remuneration; and where imitation is difficult, longevity is likely and long-term shareholder value creation is assured.

Microsoft, easyJet and Dell are three high-performing companies operating in different markets, yet all three have at least one thing in common: a winning business model.

Take easyJet, for example. The airline's business model is derived from its low-cost philosophy: easyJet attempts to cut out all non-value-adding activities as it strives to drive costs down to the absolute minimum.

The company sells directly to its customers rather than via agents and middlemen, thus saving commission costs. It also runs a ticketless operation: a customer buys a ticket, 91 per cent of which are sold over the Internet, in return for a booking reference that is then exchanged for a boarding pass at the airport check-in counter.

Most importantly, cabin crew double up as cleaners; this helps easyJet to promise a turnaround time at any airport of 30 minutes rather than the 45–60 minutes that is usually the case.

Another cost-cutting device, within the UK at least, is to use smaller airports as a base. Smaller airports, such as London Stansted, Luton or Liverpool, are cheaper to fly from than bigger airports such as Heathrow or Manchester, and also a lot less congested with shorter turnaround times for aircraft.

easyJet has no in-flight meals; a cost-saving measure that cannot be much of an inconvenience to its customers since all flights are short haul: no one will suffer from acute hunger on an easyJet flight! Nevertheless, easyJet has subcontracted catering services on its flights: customers can buy an in-flight meal and drink should they wish.

The company also has a seat-pricing policy that causes fares to rise as a flight fills up. When seats become a scarce resource, they command a higher price.

At Microsoft the winning business model is based on 'network effects'. A network effect is where a product's value to customers increases rapidly the more customers buy it (i.e. the larger the network of customers). A good example is the telephone. One telephone is no use; a few telephones are not much use, but many telephones are very useful. Network effects tend to create a strong first-mover advantage, often to the extent of creating monopolies. In most countries, single companies built up huge monopolies in telephone networks until they were broken up by regulation.

Of course, Microsoft is different from the telephone giants of the past because the network effects come from the ubiquity of its software products. If everyone uses the same word-processing software then sending and reading documents becomes easy. It makes sense to join in. In addition, by bundling software, Microsoft has been able to gain leverage from one monopoly position to create others. Microsoft has cleverly used this concept to ensure massive market share. It could be that its position is now unassailable. Whether by shrewd business decision or by uncommonly good luck, Microsoft has a fabulous winning business model.

Dell, on the other hand, seems to have found a very simple recipe for success. Traditionally, PC manufacturers built standard products that they shipped to retail outlets and distributors where they would be sold. Dell turned this process on its head. It dispensed with the retail channel entirely by trading on the Web, offering custom configurations delivered in short periods of time.

There are two other key differences between the old model and the Dell model. First, a Dell customer pays by credit card immediately for the PC before construction has even begun and, second, Dell pays the component supplier after the PC is delivered to the customer. The working capital advantages are considerable with Dell's approach – it has negative working capital. This means that it makes a very high return on capital relative to its competitors and the customers fund the company's growth.

The right capabilities and resources

Inventing a winning business model is tough – and even when you have the idea you still have to bring that idea to life. To implement your winning business model you need money, people, equipment, partners, processes, etc. We call these 'capabilities and resources'.

In the case of easyJet, what are the capabilities and resources needed to make that model fly, apart from a good deal of orange paint? Clearly, a flexible staff attitude is important. It is very difficult for BA to compete if the easyJet stewards and stewardesses are prepared to clean their own aircraft.

At Microsoft, the most valuable resource now is the strong market position in operating and application software.

In turn, at Dell, the key to its success is a genuine customer focus embedded in its direct-to-customer model, underpinned by sophisticated online systems and efficient assembly and distribution capabilities.

Dedicated leadership and strong management

The CEO cannot change a business single-handedly. What, then, are the tools the CEO uses to get others to play their part? Here we come to the two most important contributions that CEOs make to their company – management and leadership, first outlined in Part 1.

Management is 'rational action', making logical decisions, making strategy, performance management, designing processes, allocating resources, delegating responsibility, etc.

Leadership, on the other hand, is about 'symbolic action', finding ways to energize managers and staff and build commitment to deliver the company's plans, such as setting an example, telling stories, listening to stakeholders and walking the floor.

An organization that knows itself

Exceptional performance demands exceptional commitment. A team of people who know their role is not enough. All great organizations possess a range of largely intangible attributes that together drive the organization to success. These attributes include strategy, ambition, belief, capability, behaviour, focus and brand. We have collected these attributes under the banner of 'an organization that knows itself' because only when all these are truly known and understood at all levels of the company will it succeed year after year.

easyJet's corporate culture is based on 'Orangeness' (its corporate colour). easyJet's employees are 'up for it', 'passionate', 'sharp', 'mad about safety' and 'mad about cost'. 'Orange' is what makes them different.

Microsoft's culture is also suited to its goals. It is fiercely driven to maintain its (very significant) edge and concerned about competitors to the point of paranoia. The company *has* to keep pushing the frontiers of technology forward, ensuring that it 'owns' the future, almost irrespective of the cost.

Dell knows that quality of service and products are key. It is proud of its 'Soul of Dell' statement of corporate philosophy which focuses on maintaining a 'direct' relationship with its customers.

The CEOs of all three companies during their rise – Stelios Haji-Ioannou, Bill Gates and Michael Dell – have all left their own personalities indelibly marked on the culture of their company.

The expanded high-performance model depicted in Figure 13 is a complete summary of the role of the CEO. It is not, however, an all-encompassing model of everything a CEO does or should do. It is a *holistic* model: it can be applied to any task facing any CEO. To make the book complete in the sense of exhaustively covering all issues with which a CEO might be concerned – tax efficiency, IT, the appropriate role of a treasury function – is simply not possible in a book of this kind. Nor is it necessary.

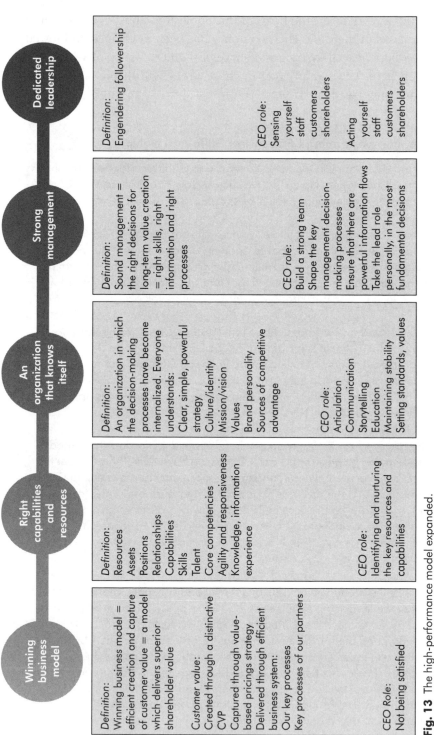

Fig. 13 The high-performance model expanded.

Source: PA analysis.

Winning business model

Right capabilities and resources

An organization that knows itself

Strong management

Dedicated leadership

Definition:
Winning business model = efficient creation and capture of customer value = a model which delivers superior shareholder value

Customer value:
Created through a distinctive CVP
Captured through value-based pricings strategy
Delivered through efficient business system:
Our key processes
Key processes of our partners

CEO Role:
Not being satisfied

Definition:
Resources
Assets
Positions
Relationships
Capabilities
Skills
Talent
Core competencies
Agility and responsiveness
Knowledge, information
experience

CEO role:
Identifying and nurturing the key resources and capabilities

Definition:
An organization in which the decision-making processes have become internalized. Everyone understands:
Clear, simple, powerful strategy
Culture/identity
Mission/vision
Values
Brand personality
Sources of competitive advantage

CEO role:
Articulation
Communication
Storytelling
Education
Maintaining stability
Setting standards, values

Definition:
Sound management = the right decisions for long-term value creation = right skills, right information and right processes

CEO role:
Build a strong team
Shape the key management decision-making processes
Ensure that there are powerful information flows
Take the lead role personally, in the most fundamental decisions

Definition:
Engendering followership

CEO role:
Sensing
yourself
staff
customers
shareholders

Acting
yourself
staff
customers
shareholders

This framework forms the heart of this book. It establishes a taxonomy of the tasks of the CEO. The taxonomy has been developed and tested with a host of well-known and successful CEOs, many of whom are quoted here. CEOs that excel in these areas will thrive, as will the company they lead.

The high-performing CEO: Jorma Ollila and Nokia

'Jorma Ollila, our CEO for over 13 years and Chairman for over six years, has built the modern Nokia that we know today,' Paul Collins, Vice-Chairman of the Nokia board (Nokia Press Release, 1 August 2005).

Nokia Corporation came into existence in its present form in 1967, as the amalgamation of three companies spanning three different industries. That it did not remain a European multi-industry conglomerate but instead became the global telecommunications company that we recognize today is down to the vision and strategy of Jorma Ollila, Nokia's CEO.

Ollila joined Nokia from Citibank in 1985 as Director of International Operations. After a stint as Senior Vice-President and CFO he was appointed President of Nokia's Mobile Phone Division. During this time he was instrumental in the pan-European adoption of the GSM standard for mobile phones. After only six years in the company he was appointed President and CEO in 1992.

The strategy that Ollila introduced changed the direction that the company was heading in: an early act as CEO was the buy-back of shares from the KOP bank to streamline management and restructure ownership. This, combined with the divestment of most of the business areas (a drastic reduction from 45 divisions in 1986 to only two business groups today), enabled the company to focus its resources into mobile phone technologies and meant that, by 1998, Nokia could justifiably claim to be the global market leader in mobile phones.

Despite the strenuous competition for a limited consumer market, Ollila's distinctive leadership style is keeping Nokia at the forefront of the field. His refusal to move the company's headquarters to a more 'traditional' location has meant the company has remained dominated by Finns, giving a unique corporate culture. The emphasis on core values, insistence on employees having a great deal of decision-making autonomy and the refusal to allow senior managers to remain in their 'comfort zone' by moving them through divisions allows Nokia to respond rapidly and effectively to new market challenges.

The constant investment in research and development (around ten per cent of group sales), constant adaptations to technology to improve productivity and regular organizational restructuring have kept both net sales and operating profit increasing year on year. In addition, Nokia leads the push to expand into previously untapped markets.

The total shareholder return (TSR) over the 13 years of Ollila's tenure at Nokia has been 43 per cent – a remarkable performance, given the rambling conglomerate with which he began.

In summary

The high-performance model, which is the subject of Part 2 of this book, describes the key tasks of the CEO.

In each of the five areas of the model, there are a relatively small number of things that a successful CEO must do – although they are not simple things to do well.

Not all CEOs are equally good at all aspects and different companies will require attention in different areas. The great CEOs correctly determine where the greatest challenges lie and – even if what is required is not a natural strength – they find a way to address these challenges.

3 A winning business model[1]

It is clear that within a single industry sector, two businesses may have radically different business models, one greatly superior to the other. For example, within the grocery sector, the multiple grocery business model is vastly superior to the corner shop model.

Unfortunately, distinguishing between a sound business model and an unsound one is extremely difficult. The dotcom 'revolution' was predicated on the idea that a whole series of new business models would invalidate the models of the old economy. With hindsight, the vast majority of these business models were completely unsound.

As a CEO, how can you be sure that the business model in your business will be more like that of a supermarket than a corner shop (or even a dotcom)?

To be confident of success, the CEO should constantly challenge the value logic behind and value delivery of the business model:

- The ability of the business to create shareholder value depends on having a business model that can efficiently *create* value for and *capture* value from other stakeholders, particularly customers.

- The soundness of any business model, however, tends to reduce over time so constant improvement is needed to ensure success.

[1] This section refers to single business models; situations involving multi-business models are covered in Appendix 1.

- The CEO must therefore continually strive to ensure that the business model will improve.

A business model that can create shareholder value

To be successful in creating shareholder value, the business model must be able to create value for the other stakeholders in the business, or they will cease to provide the input the business needs to survive. If the amount of value created for each of the other stakeholder groups is estimated, it is clear that *by far the largest slice of value created by the organization is the customer value*.

The value cascade

A value cascade diagram reveals the flows of value within a company's business system to stakeholders. Figure 14 illustrates this with a snapshot of Dell's business in 2005. It starts on the right with the total value of a product or service to the customer and ends on the left with shareholder value.

When customers buy a PC from Dell, it is because they perceive a value in the benefits that they can derive from the computer and accompany-

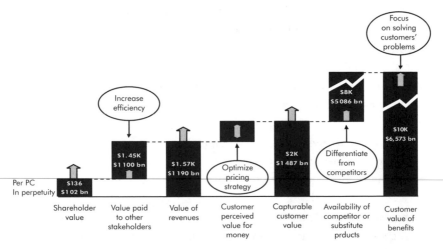

Fig. 14 Value cascade for Dell Computers (2005). Note: the upper figure represents the average value per PC sold; the lower figure is the total in perpetuity.
Source: PA analysis.

ing services offered by Dell. This value depends both on the product/ service and on the customer needs. In some instances, a single PC could be crucial to solving a problem worth millions of dollars; more often, however, the perceived value of the benefits it brings will be around $10,000.

Dell cannot hope to *capture* all of this value as revenue, because if it tried to sell a PC for $10,000, there would be competitor products that would give the customer most or all of that value but at a much reduced cost. (Theoretically, in the case of a product in a monopoly position, the monopolist *can* try to capture almost all of this value.)

In Dell's case, as in most businesses, the capturable customer value will be significantly lower than the total customer value of its products. Because there is a highly competitive market for the supply of PCs, there are well-established guidelines for PC prices that are more closely related to the costs of supply than to the value of the benefits that customers can derive. PCs are almost commodity products, and the theoretically capturable value is only around $2,000. The customer will not even be prepared to pay for *all* of the theoretically capturable value because that would leave him or her no *value for money*.

If Dell has a detailed understanding of its customers' perception of gross and capturable customer value, it can price in such a way that leaves customers perceiving excellent value for money and itself with a high level of revenue. Dell's model means that it can price for different segments with different value perceptions. On average, it can capture around $1,500 per PC.

Most of this revenue has to be paid out to other stakeholders in the business: employees, suppliers, landlords, providers of capital equipment, etc. An efficient company can sustain high levels of customer value and revenue with less need to pay cash out to other stakeholders. Dell's direct-to-customer model is highly efficient, and removes the retail margin from the value cascade; even so, around $1,450 must be paid out to other stakeholders.

Finally, the cash that remains after all other stakeholders have been paid belongs to Dell's shareholders: about $136.

The value cascade can also be used to show the expected flows of value over the lifetime of the company. In this approach, the left-hand column represents the lifetime expected value of the dividend flow to shareholders – the market capitalization of the business. In Dell's case, this is $102 billion. Similarly, the other columns reflect the total lifetime value of the value flows to other stakeholders and to customers. The total stakeholder value that Dell will create over its lifetime is truly stupendous.

Of course, not every business works on the same lines as Dell. But if we were to draw a similar diagram to Figure 14 of the value cascade for any business it would look like Dell's. The highest slice of total value would be customer value and, in the same way as for Dell, the logical place to begin building value for other stakeholders in the business is at the far right, with the customer.

This is a clear link between customer value and shareholder value, which applies to all companies. A CEO who wants to maximize shareholder value must optimize capturable customer value and efficiency.

The high-performing CEO: Michael Dell and Dell Computers

In the fiercely competitive PC market there is one company that stands out for its achievements; that company is Dell, and the man behind it, Michael Dell, founder and former CEO.

When Dell entered the PC market in the 1980s it faced IBM and HP, which dominated the industry. They possessed huge resources in contrast to Dell, who famously set up the company from his dorm at the University of Texas. Such circumstances sparked a mentality that continues to dominate the company. 'We were forced to do things based on the resources we had, that were more efficient, smarter, [and] delivered more value,' Dell explains.

Given emerging trends towards decreasing prices and commoditization, as well as the rise of the Internet, Dell's low-cost, direct-sales business model offered a superior value proposition to consumers. Mass customization exploited an increasingly standardized industry, which allowed the company to create a build-to-order manufacturing model, building PCs according to individual customer requirements. This radically reduced manufacturing costs by cutting inventories by over 20 per cent compared with competitors.

In addition, the business model radically reduced operating expenses by excluding the middleman. Focusing on the assembly and distribution of Wintel technology, Dell avoided the costs of developing alternative systems and passed on these savings to the end user. Originally dismissed by his competitors as a 'geek and a gimmick', the simple strategy pursued by Dell propelled his company to the number one position in the US computer hardware industry, and transformed the PC business. Former GE CEO Jack Welch recognizes the scale of such achievements: 'You have to just say he has done a hell of a job. No one has pulled the levers of cost, quality, and service better than Dell.'

Dell continues to rise to new challenges. The company has expanded his business model through a diversified IT portfolio as well as addressing management and organizational initiatives that aim to improve internal communication and reduce technocracy. Dell's drive and determination are perhaps best expressed through a modest attitude to his achievements so far.

Despite having an annualized ten-year TSR in excess of 50 per cent (1994–2004), he comments, 'There's a whole lot of winning left to happen. I don't really think of us as number one. You can find markets where we're number one, but I like the markets where we're not number one' (*Austin American Statesman*, May 2004).

Value creation

This value cascade enables us to understand in a slightly different way *how much* value has been created. The next question is: *how* is it created?

Figure 15 illustrates *how* a business model creates shareholder value and customer value. First of all, a proposition must be offered to a defined set of customers. This proposition generates the gross and capturable customer value described above. The pricing-strategy element of the proposition determines how much of that value is actually captured as revenue by the business.

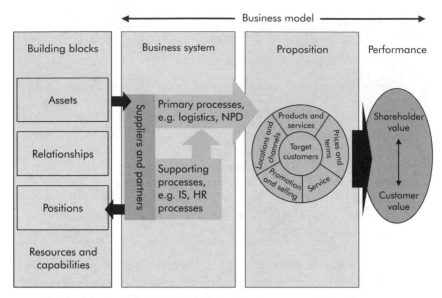

Fig. 15 Sources of competitive advantage.
Source: PA analysis.

However, in order to provide this proposition to customers, an efficient business system is required. Self-evidently, a number of primary processes are needed: for example, a manufacturing company has to purchase components or raw materials, manufacture products and deliver them to customers. A number of secondary processes are also required to manage the business and to keep it moving forward. Not all of these processes, either the primary or the secondary, need to be carried out by the business itself: there may be business partners carrying out many important processes.

The overall soundness of the business model is therefore a combination of the attractiveness of the proposition and its ability to create and capture a large amount of customer value and the efficiency of the business system that creates that capturable customer value.

It is interesting to note that when forced to trade off between efficiency and the ability to create large amounts of capturable customer value, the wise CEO will generally focus on capturable customer value: companies which do so tend to produce significantly better returns than those that focus on efficiency.

The need for improvement of business models

No business models last forever and many remain attractive only for a relatively short time.

Three factors interact to reduce the effectiveness of any business model over time. Between them, these three forces can eventually kill almost any business. The CEO is ultimately responsible for stopping that happening.

The needs and buying behaviours of the target segments may change

The needs and buying behaviours of the target segments on which the business model focuses may change over time and they can often change in a way that makes them more demanding to satisfy.

The UK dairy industry is an example of an industry where changing consumer behaviour has made it difficult to generate any kind of sustainable value. This is due to the commodity status of products such as milk, and the increased availability of these products in bulk sizes, at outlets such as supermarkets and convenience stores.

Thirty years ago, most milk was delivered to the doorstep and the dairies' customer base was large and fragmented with very little bargaining power; in those days, making a profit was relatively easy. Today, shopping patterns have changed: people buy their milk in supermarkets. The dairies' customers are large and powerful. It has become increasingly difficult to squeeze a profit out of the dairy business.

The changing market is reflected in the fortunes of the UK's dairy firms. Dairy Crest, the biggest dairy firm in the UK, has been producing smaller and smaller amounts of economic profit over the past five years. The firm is looking to move beyond the commodity products and into the higher-margin realm, at the same time steadily working to improve efficiency and capacity through plant closures and the construction of the largest 'super dairy' in the UK.

Uniq (formerly Unigate) has exited the dairy business in order to generate an economic profit, and is currently concentrating on chilled and frozen foods.

Competitors tend to observe any successful business model, and attempt to replicate or preferably trump that model

In the European airline industry, Ryanair has proved to be very successful at generating economic profits, and is competing well with the incumbent firms.

Ryanair is using a different business model to those incumbents (including British Airways) by offering cheap, point-to-point flights to secondary airports with no frills. Originally targeted at the weekend traveller, the model has proved so successful that many business travellers are also switching from the likes of BA to fly with the significantly cheaper Ryanair.

The very attractiveness of the business model spawned imitators. BA spin-off Go and KLM low-cost offshoot Buzz both competed in the no-frills low-fares market space, until bought by easyJet and Ryanair respectively.

The size and attractiveness of a segment itself may become diminished in the long term

Even if segment needs and competitor behaviour do not cause a problem, it is possible that the size and attractiveness of a segment itself may become diminished in the long term.

Henry Ford grew rich by manufacturing mass-market automobiles. The company that bears his name is still very active in this area. The market segment, however, has declined in value. The real value in the automotive industry now lies in the premium segment – e.g. Porsche, Audi, BMW – and the non-manufacturing stages in the value chain: leasing and the aftermarket.

Ensuring continual improvement

A business model will typically go through three phases.

Initially there will be *clear differentiation*. As a new concept, there will be few imitators and the firm with the new business model will obtain a huge share of a market. Growth is usually value creating and becomes the key imperative.

Once the *clear superiority* of the new model is clear, imitators will arise. Value can only be created by clear superiority in execution. In this phase consolidation and professionalization is key.

Ultimately, *commoditization* occurs – price becomes the only remaining weapon. In most cases (except for the lowest-cost producer) this means that it is no longer a winning business model.

The key to value creation is in the second phase: most good business models will spawn imitators – the key is to be able to outdo them without resorting to price as the weapon. This is a difficult trick to pull off, particularly since part of the necessary professionalization of the business may well be cost reduction.

CEOs who want to meet this challenge have a threefold role in assuring the soundness of the business model over time. They must demand proof that the logic of the current business model is sound; that it works in practice to deliver value and that it will continue to be sound in the future.

Demand proof that the logic of the current business model is sound

Before any changes to the business model are made, or before a new business model is created, the CEO should ensure that the logic of the new business model is sound (see Figure 16).

First of all, can it really *create capturable customer value*? To test this, the CEO should demand evidence that:

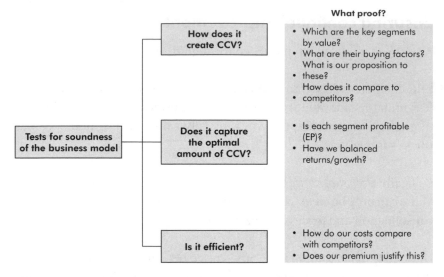

Fig. 16 Proof that the logic of the current business model is sound.
Source: PA analysis.

- The model is targeting *attractive market segments* – in the sense that these are segments in which it is possible to create value by serving them; the size of the value pools is crucial

- The *needs and consequent buying behaviours* of the target segments are well understood – through market research that is as realistic as possible

- The proposed business model has a *proposition* that addresses these needs in a *distinctive* way, including details of the competitor propositions and how they are assessed by customers.

Second, does it *capture the optimal amount* of customer value? To test this, the CEO should seek evidence that:

- The model has a *clear mechanism* for capturing a significant amount of the value created for customers (will there be charges for products, for solutions, for services, for results?)

- The amount of captured customer value exceeds the total (i.e. including capital) costs of the business model by a large margin, so that *the business will make a large economic profit*

- The proposed pricing strategy maximizes value in the long-term.

Thirdly, is the model *efficient*? The CEO should demand evidence of how:

- The costs of the new model will *compare with competitors* – assuming of course that they will also be improving

- The premium (or discount) charged by the proposed model justifies (or is justified by) the cost difference.

Demand proof that it is working in practice to deliver value

Once a model has been created, the CEO must check that it is indeed delivering shareholder value (see Figure 17).

Ultimately, a business's ability to create shareholder value depends on two factors:

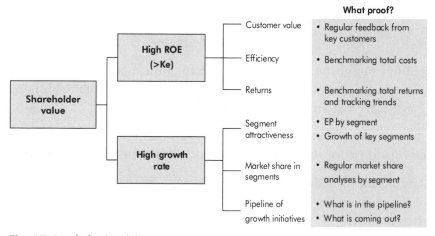

Fig. 17 Proof of value delivery.
Source: PA analysis (for a detailed explanation, see Appendix 2).

- Its ability to sustain returns to equity above the cost of its equity capital

- Its ability to grow without diluting these returns.

The returns are driven by the considerations of customer value and efficiency described above. To test their level and sustainability, the CEO needs to know:

- Does regular feedback from customers show that the proposition is still focusing on the key needs of customers; that the performance gap vs competitors, measured in terms of the business's ability to meet these needs, is widening – or at least not narrowing?

- Is the business still efficient relative to competitors, and will it remain so once competitors have made any improvements they plan?

- Are the returns above the cost of equity – or, equally, is the business generating an economic profit – and what are the trends?

To understand the likely level and profitability of future growth, the CEO should test:

- Is the growth taking place in the most valuable segments: what is the EP pool available for those who serve each segment? How fast is this pool growing (shrinking)? Is the business increasing its penetration of these EP pools?

- Does the business have a platform for future growth: is there an adequate pipeline of future growth initiatives? Do profitable business opportunities emerge from the pipeline?

Demand proof that it will continue to be sound in the future

Any business model, however sound, will eventually cease to work unless continually refreshed. Successful businesses constantly refresh their models.

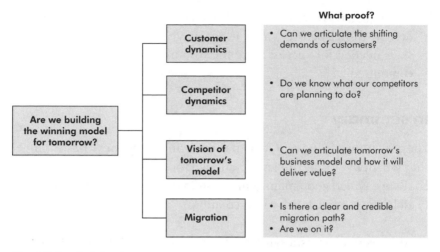

Fig. 18 Proof of development.
Source: PA analysis.

To be sure that this refreshment is happening effectively, the CEO needs to look at four things (see Figure 18):

- *Customer dynamics.* Can the managers of the business articulate clearly how customer demands are shifting and what sorts of proposition they are demanding? Do they know who tomorrow's customers will be? What unmet needs do these future customers have?

- *Competitor dynamics.* Are the managers of the business aware of competitor plans in the areas of new propositions to existing customers, refocusing of effort on to different customer segments, new business models, new channels and partnerships and do they know who tomorrow's competitors will be? How will they defeat them?

- *Vision of tomorrow's model.* Have managers articulated a clear vision of the business of tomorrow, showing how it meets the customer needs of tomorrow, how it captures value and how it will deliver efficiently?

- *Migration.* Is there a clear and credible path towards the new vision? Are there clear initiatives in place to build the new model? Are there foundations in place on which to build? Is the change being professionally managed? Are the risks clearly being managed? Have managers done similar (in terms of customers and markets, technology and organization design) things before – and, if not, have they plans to acquire the skills needed for success? Are the resources required available and committed?

In summary

There is no escaping the fact that ensuring a business has a model that will deliver is a constant challenge for the CEO. It is, however, a challenge which good management can overcome – indeed, about half of all business models are value-creating.

As this section has shown, success requires the CEO constantly to challenge the value logic behind, and value delivery of, the business model. Relentless focus on the basics – ensuring the business model captures value, recognizing the need for constant improvement of that business model and ensuring that the improvement takes place – is critical to success.

4 Right capabilities and resources

Simply being able to conceptualize a winning business model does not mean you can build it in practice. A vital role of the CEO is to identify, develop and protect the key building blocks with which future business models will be built:

- First, **identify** the few truly crucial building blocks of your future success

- Then, **develop** the building blocks you will need in future

- Always ensure that in driving performance, you **protect** the building blocks of future success.

Tesco: investment in accumulating and exploiting consumer insight

In Tesco's own words its mission is 'to create value for our customers and lifetime loyalty'.

Tesco has gained the competitive advantage in the supermarkets industry partly through significant investment in the building blocks of its winning business model, and in particular, its customer database management.

Under the guidance of Sir Terry Leahy, who became CEO in 1997, Tesco started using its loyalty card – the 'Clubcard' – as a vehicle for collecting detailed information on customers' purchases and buying behaviours. Through continued investment it has been able to expose and understand the preferences and tastes of its customers. Using a series of initiatives, including heavy spending on direct mailing, Tesco has accurately predicted trend changes and successfully introduced new products and services.

This continued investment gives Tesco the following advantages:

- Access to customer requirements, allowing Tesco to be responsive to short-term changes and accurate with its strategy for long-term growth
- Increased sales and revenues due to accurate prediction of customers' choices.

To sustain these advantages, Tesco:

- Continues to invest in the maintenance and improvement of its customer database and the quality of information held within
- Undertakes promotional activity and loyalty concepts in conjunction with its 'Clubcard', ensuring customers remain with Tesco
- Uses marketing and advertising to constantly reinforce the brand and message that Tesco puts its customers first.

The results are impressive. The investment made in the late 1990s saw pre-tax profits nearly triple in 8 years from 1997 to 2005 (£0.75 billion to £2.2 billion). Over the same period market share has grown by 24 per cent with £1 in every £8 spent in the UK being spent at Tesco.

The company has had a consistently strong level of ROI compared to the industry average. In 2000 it was 23 per cent compared to M&S with 14 per cent and Sainsbury's with 18 per cent.

Through churning profits back into the business through investment in customer database management and R&D as well as increased capacity, it has set up a strong platform for continued competitiveness and growth. This has been reflected in value-creation: over the 1994–2004 period, Tesco delivered an 18% annualized TSR to its shareholders.

Identify the few truly crucial building blocks of your future success

A definition

Before discussing how a CEO can identify the building blocks of success, it is necessary to define what we mean by building blocks.

Building blocks are of two main types: resources and capabilities. Resources can be exploited by the organization in various ways. Capabilities produce superior performance in certain important dimensions, which result from the exploitation of these resources.

Resources are divided into assets, relationships and positions:

- *Assets.* The most obvious type of resource available to managers are the assets owned by the business. This includes tangible assets such as plant, property, equipment, stock, cash, etc. Clearly, any new business model will be likely to require the use of some of these assets. It also includes intangible assets such as brands, patents, copyrights and other intellectual property, and information – for example, the profitability of individual customers.

- *Relationships with stakeholders.* Although not owned by the business, these can nevertheless constitute important building blocks. A loyal workforce committed to delivering high levels of customer service would, in most sectors, be a very valuable strategic building block. The most valuable relationships are likely to be with customers, and with employees – whether this is individually in the case of 'talent-based' industries or collectively. There are, of course, many other relationships that could be of immense value.

- *Positions.* This includes market positions, such as having a legal monopoly as was once common with utilities, or having a 40 per cent market share in an existing market, which gives access to a large market for any potential new product. It also covers broader concepts of the term such as having a reputation for dependability. This is subtly different from the brand asset that is *owned* by the organization: the reputation is merely *earned*, and is very easily lost.

These resources are all potentially valuable, but only to the extent that they create *capabilities* that allow the organization to *do* something. Unless they give rise to a superior capability to create or capture customer value efficiently, they are not contributing to a winning business model.

Very few of them will be truly critical

Most corporations have many capabilities and resources and only a few of these are really crucial to sustaining future value creation. When strategic and operational decisions are taken, having the ability to distinguish the critical capabilities and resources is essential. It is important to distinguish those that are key for the corporation to continue to create value into the future, from those that can, if necessary, be sacrificed in the interest of short-term performance. But how should a CEO make this distinction?

Capabilities and resources are key to sustaining value creation if, and only if, they are both *crucial* and *distinctive* ingredients of the business model. If they are not crucial ingredients of a future business model, they will not be crucial to the future of the organization.

Even if they *are* crucial ingredients, if these are ingredients that could easily be bought in the open market or replicated by competitors, there is little strategic advantage in preserving them.

Crucial ingredients

A winning business model is one that is more efficient at creating and capturing customer value than that of the competition. There are three possible areas in which a capability or resource may give a company an advantage:

- *Efficiency.* It may enable a company to carry out a core business process significantly more cheaply than competitors are able to, and in this way create a sustainable competitive advantage – a proprietary process, for example.

- *Creation of customer value.* If a valuable segment of the market has key customer needs that are not well met, a company with a capability or resource which would enable it to meet them effectively may well be able to take a large share of the value in that segment. The test is, therefore, to determine whether the capability or resource matches the key unmet needs of customers in a valuable segment.

- *Capture of customer value.* Usually, what one competitor can capture, so can another. But this is not always the case: with superior insight into the needs of individual customers or very small segments, a company may be able to adjust the proposition and pricing offered to these segments in a way that makes its value capture superior, even though the essence of the product and service may be no different, and even though the cost base may be no lower. A vastly superior customer database, for example, might enable this.

An asset that does not meet the test of enabling a company to be more efficient, to create more customer value or to capture more is not core, however valuable it may be. A business may own a prestigious city centre property that has been its head office for 40 years – this is a very valuable asset, but is not core. That does not imply that it must be immediately disposed of – no business consists *entirely* of core capabilities and resources – but it does mean that if circumstances presented themselves where translating this asset into cash seemed attractive, it could be done without endangering the longer-term health of the business.

Marks & Spencer: a failure to sustain investment

M&S is an example of what can go wrong when a company fails to sustain investment in the building blocks of a successful business model.

M&S pioneered a number of important concepts in retail – its returns policy, for instance – which gave it a strong competitive advantage. The company was long viewed as the star of the high street, with a brand associated with high quality and good service. These advantages meant that it was able, for a while, to avoid costs that its competitors bore: M&S did not accept credit cards; did not advertise; did not hold sales (because it did not need to). As a result, M&S's profitability was the envy of the sector.

Eventually, however, as competitors became more innovative and more professional, customers started to criticize M&S for its old-fashioned clothing range, and for not appropriately investing in marketing or staff training. What had been, for many years, a highly effective business model – which had made M&S repeatedly Britain's most admired company – gradually ceased to be competitive. Either M&S lost touch with its customers and competitors, or simply lacked the will to invest in building a new business model for the changed circumstances.

The results of these failings were significant:

- In 1999, M&S saw its profits slump from £1.16 billion to £545 million.
- Between 2000 and 2005, M&S experienced a fall in sales volumes of six per cent; over the same period, Tesco had increased sales volumes by 80 per cent while sales at Next doubled.

M&S continued to struggle for several years, until the appointment of the current CEO Stuart Rose, who has been tasked with re-focusing the business and increasing investment. In the last two years the company appears to have turned the corner: it has increased market share and significantly improved return on invested capital, though there is still considerable ground to make up.

Distinctive ingredients

Even where there is a resource, as described above, which enables the construction of a superior business model, its value is dramatically reduced if it is not unique (in which case competitors will copy quickly), or relatively easy to replicate (in which case they will still copy, but more slowly). To be strategically valuable, a capability or resource must be sustainably distinctive.

In assessing a capability or resource relative to that of a competitor it is easy to be over-optimistic. The test is whether you can be sure either that the competition does not possess the capability or resource at all, or that you have a significant (i.e. quantified and of the order of at least 20 per cent) performance advantage in relation to the capability in question.

Even more tempting is to assume that a lead is a permanent lead. Very few sources of competitive advantage are sustainable indefinitely: unless it is absolutely clear that they are insurmountable barriers, it is wise to assume that any lead can be eroded over a five-year period.

Kmart is a salutary example. The US retailer pioneered large-scale multiple grocery chains in the US. It made a lot of money applying the capabilities it had developed across an ever-larger number of stores. Unfortunately, these capabilities were not sustainably superior. Kmart was outperformed by archrival Wal-Mart, and even forced into Chapter 11 bankruptcy protection for a period.

Develop the building blocks you will need in future

Having identified the key building blocks of future business models, the next step is to be sure that they are developed.

Follow the logic of the future business model

The business model itself is the guide to this development. Start with the proposition for the future business model, then determine what capabilities are required – for example, performance characteristics of future products, required service levels and the cost position needed for the new business model to be value-creating.

Based on the assessment of these capabilities, a CEO can determine the resources required to construct the business model.

If a company needs to be able to deliver products to customers at three hours' notice, then it needs access to a logistical system with warehouses situated close by – the resource needed might be a series of warehouses owned by the company, or it might be a relationship with a logistics partner, plus a communications mechanism enabling the company and its partner to respond almost instantly to customer demand. Such a model could almost certainly be created – but it is hard to see how to make it sustainably differentiated.

Or a company might need to cool liquids using half the energy of existing approaches; in which case it will need access to new technology. R&D leading to a proprietary cooling technology, or else licensing-in a technology developed elsewhere, might create the resource needed. In the first case, the model might be sustainably different; in the second, obtaining an exclusive licence might be prohibitively expensive.

Plan to develop or acquire unique capabilities and resources

Once the capability and resource needs are clear, the next step is to find an economic way of developing them in a way that will be hard to replicate.

The easiest way to do this is organically: if the resources are already at least partly in place, the cost of replication for a competitor is likely to be far higher. It is far harder for competitors to replicate what you *are* than what you *do*.

When Virgin decided to branch out from its then core business of retailing records and CDs into flying transatlantic aeroplanes, its competitors, the other retailers, could have copied the *action* but they would not have replicated the *result*. Crucial to the success of Virgin Atlantic was the brand and associated reputation of Virgin. This brand is clearly of great value in creating new business models, but is idiosyncratic and linked to the personality of one man – CEO Richard Branson – to such an extent that it is almost impossible to replicate. Virgin, of course, takes great care to develop the brand – but its success in doing so is more a function of its history than of its current skill in brand management, and this is what makes the Virgin brand so valuable.

Assets and resources can also be acquired, some much more easily than others: a brand can be bought – at a price – but a reputation cannot, a technology can be bought but a culture cannot, tangible assets can all be bought – but some organizations have the ability to derive more value from them than others; that ability cannot be bought.

Thinking through the best approach to development and acquisition of the resources and competences needed for future success is a key role of top management and of the CEO in particular.

Ensure that in driving performance, you nevertheless protect the building blocks of your future success

It is all very well talking of future business models and future value created. The problem for CEOs is that they are under intense pressure to deliver value here and now. Driving current performance is a key role of the CEO, and it frequently requires taking tough decisions.

The most difficult area is where the protection of the building blocks for the future is sub-optimizing current performance: what should the CEO do? The answer is hard but simple: do not sacrifice the future to achieve short-term success unless the very existence of the firm is under threat. Very few of the capabilities and resources will be truly critical – be absolutely clear which are the few critical ones; it will be far easier to decide what to sacrifice.

Do not cut or outsource the building blocks

It might be possible to report higher profits by reducing R&D spend, but that is not a good enough reason for doing it. Of course, if there is R&D spend which is not value creating, deal with it as mercilessly as with any other kind of waste.

It may take a tough and detailed review to determine whether R&D spend is or is not value-creating, including at least the following factors: track record of delivery of profitable new products and ROI on R&D spend; current R&D pipeline and prospects and effectiveness of R&D processes.

If R&D spend promises to create value by contributing to an important future business model, however, the economics of cutting are unsound.

A similar issue applies to outsourcing: the costs of an operational process are very clear; the value created for customers is usually not. If a company underestimates the impact of the non-cost factors, it may be tempted to outsource and – at least in the first few years – may see costs fall significantly. However, if that company has traded its ability to create customer value for a lower-cost base, it will have inadvertently moved towards a strategy of being the lowest-cost producer. This is, of course, a valid strategy providing the company *can* be the lowest-cost producer, but if not (and only one player in any market can do it) competing on price will be highly destructive of value.

Make sure that others also protect the building blocks – especially the softer ones

Cost reduction and outsourcing are usually major strategic issues that will be clearly visible to the CEO. However, there may be other issues less visible but in aggregate equally important – the equivalent decisions will be delegated to other managers. These managers must be aware of the need to protect these crucial building blocks. The danger is particularly clear in the case of the softer resources, where the value is most easily underestimated.

For example, the loyalty and commitment of a large number of customer-facing staff is something that can have a huge impact on the long-term economics of a business. This loyalty and commitment is a resource that is easily dissipated – indeed, it requires a constant effort on the part of a large number of managers at a variety of levels to sustain it.

Some of these efforts may also be in conflict with short-term perform-ance. The CEO, therefore, needs to ensure that all the managers under-stand the value of this resource and are committed to maintaining it.

Carphone Warehouse: long-term gain at short-term cost

Carphone Warehouse is a good example of a company that understands the need to protect the essential building blocks of its business model, even though it may be costly in the short term.

Buying the right mobile phone is an increasingly complex decision, and one on which many consumers value advice: they are not prepared to pay for it, but if it is offered, they exhibit a clear preference.

By combining their pledge 'find your handset cheaper and we'll refund the difference – guaranteed' with sound advice, Carphone Warehouse has created a highly attractive offer.

Sustaining this advantage is costly in the short term: the company invests four times the industry average in staff training; a proportion of profits is set aside for new training initiatives each year; alongside its staff-training investment, Carphone Warehouse has invested heavily in its IT infrastructure and trains its staff in any changes; and the pledge itself is costly.

Despite these obvious costs, Carphone Warehouse's results are proof that its continued investment in sustaining and reinforcing its business model is a sound strategy.

For the financial year 2004–2005 the company reported increased sales volumes of 27 per cent, with economic profit increasing by 29 per cent (£545 million to £705 million). Carphone Warehouse has also seen an increase of 17.3 per cent in new connections in the UK. In 2000, after embarking on its focused investment in staff training, the ROI at the company was 88 per cent.

In summary

Companies cannot afford to stand still. They may have a winning business model but, if they wish to preserve any advantage that it provides, they must continue to refine and improve the business model. This creates a demand for the building blocks of future success. These building blocks are constructed from resources and capabilities.

When it comes to the building blocks there are three important steps for CEOs to remember.

- **Identify** the few truly crucial building blocks of future success

- **Develop** them

- **Protect** them.

It is the CEO's responsibility to nurture the capabilities and resources the organization will need to do this. It is a difficult task.

Dell's key advantages

Dell's competitive advantage stems from the power of its direct-to-customer business model. This model gives Dell two key advantages:

- **Customer value** – Dell is able to be more responsive to customers in both the short term (which manifests in better customer service) and the long term (which manifests in products and services which succeed in the market)
- **Efficiency** – both in terms of cost and capital requirements, Dell's model is superior to that of its competitors.

To sustain these advantages, Dell invests in two main ways:

- In reinforcing the business model, e.g. by continuing to invest in customer services; in R&D (which has averaged ten per cent of revenue) – which is clearly a big drain on short-term profitability – and in further improving efficiency by aggressively stripping out costs that do not relate to the essential building blocks of future business models.
- In extending and exploiting the power of the business model – e.g. by extending the scope of products (from PCs to peripherals, systems and software), of customers (from individuals to SMEs and large companies and governments) and of markets (from the US to the rest of the world).

The results have been outstanding: annual growth is running at about 20 per cent; market share increases by more than one per cent annually; return on invested capital is very high – at least 60 per cent, however you calculate it.

As a result, Dell has been the best performer among our sample of large companies in terms of shareholder value creation over the last ten years.

5 Dedicated leadership

Most research on the subject of leadership focuses on traits. What personality traits make a successful leader? What traits do Bill Gates and Winston Churchill have in common? All of this is interesting and potentially valuable to those involved in *selecting* CEOs, but not very useful to those who *are* or *want to be* CEOs.

If you have chosen to read this book it is probably because you *are* a CEO, *expect* to become a CEO or have a burning passion one day to *become* a CEO. You are not going to undergo a personality transplant. You are who you are. Focusing on your character traits is therefore of limited practical value.

So, should those who are short of a trait or two in the leadership stakes withdraw from CEO candidacy? Of course not: CEOs are judged on what they do, not on their personality. For example, an oft-attributed common trait of great leaders is charisma. In 2002, Henry Tosi, McGriff Professor of Management at the University of Florida, led a study that looked at the charisma of 59 CEOs of Fortune 500 companies and investigated the correlation with firm performance. The study found that there was no link between the perceived charisma of the CEOs and improved performance. The trick, therefore, is to know what a CEO in the role of leader should *do*. One important role of leaders is to engender followership and as a result it is essential to understand the things that CEOs can do to make this happen.

What is followership and what actions engender it?

You won't find 'followership' in the *Oxford English Dictionary*, but it neatly describes what the leader is trying to generate – the commitment of the individuals in any organization to the aims of its leader. The title of CEO on its own does not provide any long-lasting ability to draw followers. The authority of the title is strengthened or diminished by the specific actions that the CEO takes.

Part 1, Section 3 discussed the difference between management and leadership; the difference between taking decisions and creating action. Leadership is, for the large part, symbolic. Good leaders take actions that do not in themselves have an immediate bearing on the efficacy of an organization and its ability to satisfy stakeholders but, over a period of time, make those stakeholders feel more closely aligned with the objectives of that organization and therefore take the actions needed to achieve those objectives.

Tim Parker, CEO of the AA, the UK's former Automobile Association, put it well when he said: 'Leadership is about reducing the gap between the leader and the led.'

The high-performance leadership model

Our discussions with leading CEOs confirm this focus on action. Leadership is an intensely **practical** issue. Good leaders **do** the right things: they take the right **symbolic actions.**

There are four groups who will be affected by a CEO's symbolic actions: the shareholders, the customers, the staff and, of course, the CEO.

Why the CEO? Because the CEO is under the microscope, watched at work, even outside work. CEOs must understand, believe, like and be in control of themselves. As leader, CEOs are the standard-bearers and standard-setters for their company. This means that they cannot say 'do as I say, not as I do' and retain any credibility. They cannot snub a customer and expect their employees to show real concern for customers, for example.

For each group – shareholders, staff, customers and CEO – the leader must find a way to master both *acting* and *sensing*. Sensing is about under-

	You	Your staff	Your customers	Your shareholders
Sensing	Knowing yourself	Keeping your ear to the ground	Being a customer	Being a shareholder
Acting	Being yourself	Walking the walk	Getting behind the counter	Visible alignment

Fig. 19 The content of leadership.
Source: PA analysis.

standing what needs to be done. Acting is about taking action – doing what needs to be done (see Figure 19).

Leading yourself

Knowing yourself

As part of the research for this book we talked to a headhunter of CEOs, Rae Sedel of Russell Reynolds Associates. We asked her what she looked for in a CEO. She replied that the first thing she looked for was 'a CEO that knows him or herself. Because a CEO who does not understand himself or herself can be a liability. The perfect CEO is an impossible dream. But a CEO who understands their own strengths and weaknesses has information vital to building the perfect team.'

Sedel recalled a prospective CEO who was rude to the doorman at the offices of Russell Reynolds Associates, rude to the receptionist and rude to the person who brought the coffee into the waiting room. The candidate at interview then proceeded to tell Sedel how he saw himself as a people person.

Being yourself

Are you happy *being* yourself? The CEOs we spoke to all agreed that it was imperative to be yourself. In the words of Gareth Davies, CEO of Imperial Tobacco: 'The job of chief executive is demanding and complex enough without having to live a lie.'

Think of the CEO communicating and the image of the charismatic leader standing on stage, setting staff emotions on fire, springs to mind.

Why? Such fervour rarely lasts. The job of the CEO is to 'set the tone'. This requires little oratory and indeed, in extreme cases, can be done almost entirely with the aid of email. The keys to good communication here are clarity of thought and consistency. The CEO's message needs to be understood and agreed by almost everyone, so clear and compelling logic is essential. Consistency is a must as even the most brilliant speaker loses impact if the message changes with the wind.

Leading your staff

Keeping your ear to the ground

It follows that, to lead well, it is important to know how those you wish to lead feel and think. CEOs agree that this is crucial but tend to use different methods to achieve their aim.

Joseph Wan is the CEO of Harvey Nichols – an internationally renowned chain of UK department stores. He has been CEO for ten years and over that time has achieved his target of doubling profit every five years. Wan uses four mechanisms to listen to his workforce. First, he asks his direct reports to comment on staff issues every week. Second, staff representatives give their views at a staff council. Third, Wan reads the exit interviews conducted with departing staff by the HR department. Last, and certainly not least, he believes in observation. He walks around the store every day. This allows Wan to experience the mood and attitude of his workforce at firsthand.

Konosuke Matsushita, the founder of Matsushita Electrical, was also a great believer in 'walking the floor'. Matsushita's approach was a particularly enlightened one, coming as it did during the 1930s, an era dominated by Frederick Taylor's scientific management which paid scant regard to the feelings of employees.

Speaking to senior managers within the company, Matsushita said: 'I don't want you to just hide yourself away in that factory. You've got to know the points of view of your salespeople and the customers, and let what you observe be reflected in your work.'

Making the rounds of department stores, Matsushita would present himself and his business card not only to the store manager, but also at each electric appliance department, handing over cards to everyone he met. He would make a point of asking the shop assistants what the key concerns of customers were.

Walking the walk

Walking the walk means setting an example. What message does the CEO send by flying first class while everyone else flies economy? What message does the CEO send by being picked up by the chauffeur while everyone else is queuing for the bus? On arriving at British Telecom, Ben Verwaayen found an executive canteen, an executive washroom and even an executive lift. Within the first few weeks they were gone. The symbolic power of these actions is immense.

Showing the staff what is important to the firm is vital. If a key component of your competitive advantage is the excellence of your customer service then the CEO should talk to customers. If the key is cost leadership then that attitude to cost should go all the way up to the CEO's office.

The high-performing CEO: Sir John Bond and HSBC

In 2004, Sir John Bond received a lifetime achievement award, recognizing his remarkable contribution to the success of the bank he joined in 1961 when he was just 20 years old. Embedded in the profitable and bold strategy of HSBC are the personal traits of Sir John: resilience, adaptability and innovation. Such characteristics underwrite the calculated opportunism that has driven a sequence of acquisitions transforming the company into one of the world's top three banking groups. Asked about the deals he states: 'We had the choice of going forwards or backwards and when faced with that choice HSBC unerringly goes for the forwards option. We are not quitters, we have never been quitters, never will be quitters.' Such statements unearth quiet determination beneath the modesty and even self-deprecation that Sir John has become known for. It also highlights the links between the personality of the bank and the man that runs it.

Among the deals that he presided over were the $9.85 billion acquisition of private banking group, Republic New York, and the $11 billion takeover of Credit Commercial de France, just one year later. Most risky was the controversial buy-out of consumer finance group Household International in 2002.

Bond's strategy is rooted in a fundamental belief in shareholder value, a responsibility that encouraged him to seek out new market opportunities despite investors' pessimism over the Household deal. This raised concerns as it introduced HSBC into lower-income consumer segments, with risky credit ratings. Bond's foresight proved profitable, however, as the bank delivered a record £5.1 billion profit for the first half of 2004, with Household doubling the group's total earnings in the USA, which account for 34 per cent of HSBC profits.

In addition to focusing on the US market, Bond pursued growth in developing markets, finalizing a deal with the Bank of Communications that gave HSBC the biggest footprint of any foreign bank on the Chinese mainland.

Finally, his commitment to shareholders was reflected in his frugal attitude to spending, which extended to his own travel in economy class for European flights. It is this combination of opportunism and conservatism that breeds the unique model of success that Sir John Bond has created at HSBC and that has enabled the banking group to prosper through highs and lows within the industry. The ten-year annualized TSR from 1994 to 2004 was an impressive 18 per cent.

Leading your customers

Being a customer

The CEO must understand the customer. The CEO is far too powerful to misunderstand the needs of the customer.

Gareth Davies is the CEO of one of the largest tobacco firms in the world. He smokes 40 cigarettes a day.

In 1970, some 7.6 million people visited the Matsushita Pavilion during the world exposition held in Osaka. A few days after the fair opened, the pavilion supervisors watching the television monitors aimed at the entrance area were startled to see the figure of Matsushita himself standing patiently in the line of visitors waiting to be admitted. Flustered by this unexpected and unannounced visit, the pavilion's second in command rushed out to greet him, asking Matsushita why he was standing there.

Matsushita replied, 'Oh, I just thought I'd find out for myself how much time people had to wait before they could get in.'

Getting behind the counter

A fantastic way of understanding what customers think is to get into the front line – behind the counter. Bob Marshall of British Airways would regularly check out the front line by getting behind the check-in counter.

Ben Verwaayen explained that he once spent a day in the call centre. 'I realized I wasn't capable of answering the phone, even with a script. Now I have more respect for the people that work there. You must have respect for people in all layers of the organization – for their professionalism and their personality.'

Additionally, Verwaayen is famous for making his email address public and answers customers himself, copying in the appropriate manager. A customer once sent Verwaayen an email saying it was harder to get him on the phone than the Pope. Verwaayen phoned him, saying, 'Hello, it's the Pope here, I'll just get you the Chief Executive of BT.'

Leading your shareholders

Being a shareholder

A sizeable shareholding clearly helps the CEO understand the needs of the shareholder. If the CEO begins to wish that he had his wealth in government bonds you can bet your pension the company is not providing adequate returns on equity.

A number of CEOs we spoke to said that the CEO should have a sizeable amount of their wealth in the company they run. Gareth Davies of Imperial Tobacco went further: 'Virtually all my wealth, excluding the house I live in, is in Imperial Tobacco shares, around 95 per cent of my total wealth. I believe that the rest of the executive team should have similar percentages of their wealth tied up in the shares of Imperial Tobacco.'

Additionally, with a strong staff equity scheme the staff should begin to feel part of the game too. Gareth Davies continues: 'I get the greatest satisfaction from knowing that there are people on the factory floor who have made a significant amount of money from purchasing our shares.'

Visible alignment

Having wealth tied up in shares is important but it is equally important to let everyone know. The obvious place to start is the annual report, but too often the directors' shareholdings are in a table at the back. This should be on the front page – how much the CEO gained, or lost, by being a shareholder; how the CEO plans to increase the value of those shares in coming years and what the existing businesses will contribute to the creation of shareholder value. Warren Buffett is very clear each year about the proportion of his and his family's wealth tied up in Berkshire Hathaway shares (around 99 per cent according to his *Owners' Manual*). As he says, 'We eat our own cooking.'

CEOs spend on average 20 per cent of their time in investor relations. This is, surely, bizarre. The primary job of the CEO is to oversee the creation of intrinsic value, not run around New York and London trying to convince analysts that they will soon see an increase in whatever measure the analysts have decided to focus on: EBITDA, EPS, like-for-like sales, etc. Most CEOs seem resigned to this. Maybe it is time for CEOs to fight back. After all, one of the most successful CEOs in history, Warren Buffett, only spends one weekend a year talking to Berkshire Hathaway shareholders. And they come to him.

In summary

There is no leader without followers. One of the key roles of the CEO, therefore, and one of the toughest challenges, is to engage the commitment of the stakeholders in following the vision and goals set out by the CEO.

The high-performance leadership model can help corporate leaders meet that challenge. Through sensing and acting wisely in relation to staff, customers, shareholders and, equally important, yourself, you can provide effective and dedicated leadership.

6 Strong management

Another key role of the CEO is to ensure that management throughout the organization is sound.

Management should be defined by the decisions that it makes. Adopting this logic, it is self-evident that sound management is crucial to business performance and conversely that businesses without sound management run an unacceptable risk of failure. Unfortunately, it is equally clear that any CEO who attempts to become personally involved in every decision will be drowned in detail.

Any CEO who relies on people within the organization to take sound decisions must address four factors: people, values, processes and information. This poses the question: what should be the role of the CEO in ensuring the soundness of management decision-making?

The role of the CEO is to control the overall direction of decision-making, without attempting to take every decision personally. Striking this balance requires the CEO to:

- Create a team of people whose decision-making the CEO is comfortable to rely on

- Shape the key management decision-making processes explicitly to guide the decisions of this team and others in line with maximizing long-term performance

- Ensure that there are powerful information flows that keep all managers grounded in the reality of the business

- Take the lead role, personally, in the most fundamental decisions facing the organization.

While there is no way that the CEO can be *certain* that all the decisions taken by others (or even the decisions the CEO takes personally) will be right, there is ample evidence that CEOs who address the four points above manage to sustain higher long-term performance.

Building a strong team

The first important task of the CEO is to create a strong team. It is no less important, however, to continue to build the strength of the team through ongoing *development* and careful *succession planning*. Indeed, great CEOs are often judged partly by reference to the performance of their successors.

Key considerations in determining the membership of the team include the match of skills and abilities – in particular, the CEO must be aware of and compensate for any personal weaknesses; the ability to deliver results, not just to create great plans; a willingness to commit to the long-term performance of the business; the ability and willingness to work as part of the team; and integrity.

Assessing these characteristics is far from easy, and decisions about team composition are, therefore, hard to get right. Recruiting externally is no panacea: failure rates are in excess of 40 per cent, according to US-based HR consulting firm Manchester Inc., which is embarrassing, costly and demoralizing. Nevertheless, if there is no suitable internal candidate, CEOs should not hesitate to opt for a 40 per cent risk against certain failure.

In describing the attributes he looks for in someone he hires, Warren Buffett lists intelligence, energy and integrity. 'If they don't have the last one, the first two will kill you. Think about it, if they don't have integrity, you want them to be dumb and lazy.'

To some extent, these points apply to team building at all levels. The key difference in the case of a CEO is that there are fewer constraints: you do not have to recruit from within; you are not bound to follow the recommendations of HR – and therefore there are fewer excuses. After one year in the post, the CEO is responsible for the team composition as well as its performance. If you have not got the best possible team, as CEO you have only yourself to blame.

As well as determining the composition of this team, the CEO is also responsible for its performance and therefore must take *personal* responsibility for the skills and capability development of the team as well as the performance management of its members and for the way in which they are remunerated.

If the CEO can only perform well when supported by a strong team, the same is equally true of all other managers. Many of the comments above, therefore, apply to managers at all levels in the organization.

The high-performing CEO: William (Bill) H. Gates and Microsoft

In common with many other founder-CEOs, Bill Gates maintained a high level of control over Microsoft throughout its exceptional growth of the past two decades. Unlike many of his contemporaries, Gates was both able to cope initially with the demands that such a high level of involvement places on the CEO and, when his limits were reached, was able to recognize and arrive at a solution.

During the initial phase, Gates' management model overlaid the small focused groups required for software development with tight financial controls, placing him in overall control of these projects and the overall strategy of the business. This approach was highly effective for Microsoft's growth phase as it enabled what were still relatively modular products to be built on time and, crucially, on budget. However, as the complexity of Microsoft's operations grew in line with the growth in complexity of the products they were developing, the bureaucracy started to become inhibitive and Microsoft started to falter. In fact Gates' split focus is seen by many as the reason behind the delay in the company's response to the opportunities of the Internet.

Gates' response to this was to both instigate the federalization of the company's business units, and to delegate the operational management of Microsoft to Steve Ballmer, allowing himself to concentrate on overall strategy.

This increased autonomy of the business units alleviated management overhead and also helped re-engage the senior managers of the business units, many of whom had made considerable fortunes since the early days but had been disenfranchised by the bureaucratic Microsoft.

This change of business model has helped to sustain the performance of Microsoft, with revenues increased by more than 50 per cent from 2001 to 2005, despite a technological and economic downturn. In addition, Microsoft has a good product pipeline that Ballmer attributes to the company's culture and reduction in bureaucracy: 'We have a great culture that promotes criticism ... Our company has to be a company that enables its people ... We've got more empowered, innovative, creative people than any other company in the world.' Such achievements contribute to shareholder value, with the annualized TSR enjoyed by Microsoft shareholders since December 1994 at 23 per cent, a truly astonishing track record.

Shaping management decision-making to maximize long-term performance

How can the CEO shape decision-making processes to guide other managers towards optimizing long-term performance? In order to answer this very difficult question, we surveyed the chairmen, chief executives and chief financial officers of the leading quoted companies worldwide.[1]

The most striking finding from this survey was that the companies that sustain higher performance over the long term are those that adopt management processes explicitly focusing on maximizing long-term shareholder value.

By putting in place and rigorously enforcing such processes, CEOs can double performance over their period of tenure.[2] We call this managing for shareholder value (MSV) (see Figure 20).

[1] *2002 Survey on Managing for Shareholder Value*, PA Consulting Group.
[2] The average tenure of CEOs over the past 20 years has been around seven to eight years. Average tenure as a CEO declined from 9.5 years in 1995 to 7.3 years in 2001 (Booz Allen Hamilton study released 17 March, 2002).

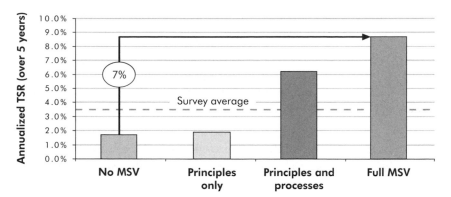

Fig. 20 TSR effects of managing for shareholder value.
Source: *Managing for Shareholder Value 2002 International Survey Report*, PA Consulting Group.

There are three key management processes in which the CEO should take a personal interest to ensure that they are indeed aligned with maximizing long-term shareholder value:

• Strategic planning

• Performance management and remuneration

• Investor relations.

Because the survey also showed that only about 20 per cent of companies align these processes effectively, it is worth spending a little time to explore what true alignment looks like in each case.

Strategic planning

Most CEOs, when asked, will agree that the overarching objective of management is to maximize the long-term shareholder value of the business. But when you examine the strategic planning processes in place in most organizations you find that they are not aligned with supporting that objective.

In fact in most cases they focus on one of two things: *maximizing long-term revenues* – for example, a strategic planning process which sets out to establish global leadership or to maximize market share; or *maximizing short-term profits* (usually operating profits) – for example, many strategic processes used in multi-divisional businesses.

Not surprisingly, the result is that these companies deliver less in the way of long-term shareholder value than those companies whose approaches to strategy are value based.

The importance of the strategic approach must not be underestimated. An average business will have replaced its entire balance sheet with new assets in seven years.

For a company, strategy is like DNA – it can control asset allocation. After seven years, a company is truly responsible for where it has allocated its capital – and for the returns it is getting on that capital.

A typical strategy process will go through the stages shown in Figure 21. Some of the keys to success at each stage are highlighted below.

Foundations

For a value-based approach to strategy formulation, there are some foundations that must first be in place.

First and foremost, the organization must explicitly state that its over-arching objective is to maximize long-term shareholder value. It should then set a goal that relates to this objective: a goal for long-term total shareholder return (TSR) that the management team intends to deliver.

The next step is to conduct a value-based analysis of the status quo to understand where in the business value is being created now: in which business units, in which geographies, in which product lines and, ideally,

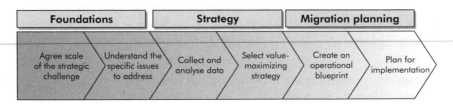

Fig. 21 A typical strategy process.
Source: PA analysis.

in which customer segments. This analysis on its own is usually extremely powerful for the simple reason that most businesses have about half of their shareholders' capital tied up in value-diluting or value-destroying activities. When they decide how to reinvent themselves, they need to know what is worth reinventing

As well as understanding *where* value is created it is important also to understand *why* it has been created in strategic terms – are you creating value because you are in a market which is so attractive that every player in that market is creating value; or is it that, despite the fact that the market is deeply unattractive, you have such a strong competitive advantage that you are able to create value anyway?

Next, you need to understand what has most impact on changing that value. Would it be worth more to improve customer retention by three per cent or to add one point to the gross margin? Is an extra two points of market share worth more or less than an extra one per cent on the bottom line?

Finally, you must agree the size of the gap between the status quo and what is needed to hit your long-term goals.

With this foundation in place, it becomes relatively simple for managers to identify the key issues that must be addressed to maximize the value of the business, and to set out specific challenges, specific strategic options and specific hypotheses that need to be tested in order to select the value-maximizing strategy.

Strategy

At this point, there are two schools of thought as to how to resolve these issues. One approach is to convene the management team in a pleasant country house hotel and to spend a couple of days debating the issues until a consensus is reached. The other is to set up a hit squad of able managers with a combination of business and financial expertise to conduct a rigorous analysis of the issues, hypotheses and options with the aim of enabling the top team to make a value-based selection of the best strategic option open to them.

In practice, the best strategy passes three tests: it must be *feasible*; it must make *economic sense* and it must be a strategy that the organization is prepared to *commit* to delivering.

Without detailed analysis, the strategy adopted by top management runs the risk of passing the third test without adequate reference to the first two. Many exciting, dramatic and radical strategies – which are ultimately unsuccessful – result from this approach. Nevertheless, we have heard chairmen say: 'I don't really mind what strategy the CEO chooses – as long as I am convinced that he is really committed to it.' This overstates the value of commitment.

It is equally dangerous to understate the value of commitment. Without the heavy involvement of top management, the strategy may be well researched – and even right – but it ignores the commitment test and is very unlikely to be driven through to a successful implementation. Many 'brilliant' strategies are still sitting on shelves for this reason.

To be successful, a strategy process must therefore contain a judicious mix of the country house and hit squad styles.

Importantly, when it comes to selecting the right strategy, there are two obvious but rarely practised points to bear in mind.

If there is only one strategic option being considered, you cannot be sure that there is not a much better option than the one on offer. This means that to be confident of doing a good job you must consider three or four plausible options. The plausible aspect is important. When Henry Kissinger was Secretary of State of the United States, he complained that his advisers would always present him with three options for consideration, but the first would be tantamount to surrender to the Soviet Union while the second would inevitably result in large-scale thermonuclear conflict, leaving him with no choice but to run with the third.

If you select a strategy on a basis other than its impact on long-term shareholder value, it is unlikely to be the value-maximizing strategy. In particular, selecting on the basis of impact on operating profit or earnings per share can lead to dangerously poor decisions.

The best strategic option will meet the following tests:

- With hindsight it will usually seem obvious, though at the start of the process it was far from being clear and agreed

- It will use the distinctive resources and capabilities of the business to create a hard-to-copy business model serving an attractive market or segment.

- This business model will be clearly superior in creating and capturing customer value, and it will be efficient in doing so.

- The strategy will build on existing areas and means of value creation, and will have a higher Net Present Value (NPV) than any other option.

Migration

The final step, but by no means any less important, is to ensure successful implementation. This requires a high-level strategy to be translated into a concrete operational blueprint of how the future business must look.

In many cases – but by no means all – this new blueprint will look very different from the way the business currently runs. If this is the case then migration to the new state will be difficult and complex and a very careful assessment of the implementation issues and change management issues (to bring people along) becomes very important. A detailed implementation plan must be drawn up and fully costed, *by those who must implement it*, before the final business case is produced, which leads to sign-off for the new strategy.

Our research showed that companies whose approach to strategy is truly value based deliver around seven per cent per annum higher TSR than those without a value-based approach. Interestingly, this result was consistently found in each of the 12 major countries we surveyed.

Aligning performance management and remuneration

The next key process is performance management and remuneration: the way in which performance is measured, tracked and rewarded over time. This is one of the key areas of corporate governance, and is crucial to ensuring that the strategy will be delivered.

It is a truism of management that you get what you measure. It is therefore very important to ensure that the measures in place in the organization are value based. In most organizations, our survey showed that they were not. With financial measures, the majority of businesses still run principally on operating profit; some also focus on return on sales or return on capital employed. Focusing on any of these measures can drive managers away from maximizing shareholder value; in fact, we believe that in many organizations today, managers are *prevented* from managing for shareholder value, even if they had wanted to do so.

One value-based measure of performance is economic profit: a simple measure that tells managers, often for the first time, whether they are making or losing money. Not all managers, and certainly not all staff, are actually profit-responsible, however. Many are responsible for very important issues and decisions that nevertheless cannot be translated directly into profit terms. It is therefore very important to understand what are the key *non-financial* drivers of shareholder value. These are called value drivers and a management team which truly understands the five most important value drivers as well as having a clearer picture

	CEO	Manager
Promises	Resources: –People –Financial –Intellectual Freedom to act (within limits)	To hit an agreed value-creation target To deliver specific strategic milestones by specific deadlines To safeguard the long-term health of the business
And expects in return	Delivery of promised value Accurate assessment of past progress and future prospects Compliance with corporate values	The resources, authority and support needed to deliver, so long as they keep their own promises

Fig. 22 Performance contracts.
Source: PA analysis.

of economic profit in their business is in a stronger position to create shareholder value than one without this understanding.

Performance management

Key to delivery of strategy is the concept of a performance contract in which the CEO contracts with the management of each part of the business as shown in Figure 22.

The creation of the contract should take place as the strategy is signed off. Regular, probably quarterly, reviews against the performance contract are then the key to ensuring delivery.

Making performance contracting work

When John McGrath was CEO of Diageo, he introduced both performance contracting and the idea of BHAGs (Big Hairy Audacious Goals – an idea derived from the book *Built to Last*).

The senior executives all signed up to a demanding set of economic profit (EP) targets. One of these executives, Jack Keenan, responsible for the Spirits Division at Diageo-owned United Distillers & Vintners, came to McGrath, explaining, 'Having done the analysis in more detail, I can see that to hit the target we would need to capture 80 per cent of the EP in the entire spirits market. To be practical, I think we should reconsider.' McGrath demurred, saying, 'I am not keen to start backing away from commitments – go and have another look at what you could do.' Keenan duly looked again, and found that in a neighbouring market – the alco-pops – was a huge pool of EP. This discovery led him to launch Smirnoff Ice, one of Diageo's most successful products.

Reward

As well as tracking value creation, it is important to reward it; and therefore these measures must be the basis on which managers are rewarded. As well as using the right – i.e. value-based – measures, three other factors turn out to be very important in driving long-term shareholder value.

First, the bonus must relate to long-term value-creation performance, not short-term profit performance; this requires some form of bonus deferment or banking to make sure that managers do not squander the long-term health of the business in pursuit of apparent short-term gains.

Second, managers should be encouraged, by the bonus system, to build up large ownership of shares in the business (not options, which have been proven statistically to correlate with far worse performance).

Third, the ratio of variable to fixed pay should be far higher than is common in many European businesses.

Best-practice remuneration is depicted in Figure 23.

The total reward is made up of base salary and bonus: the balance of these should be tilted as far as possible towards bonus. The bonus itself should be calculated in two stages: first, the calculation of a pool that relates to the value delivered by all or part of the business; second, the calculation of the individual allocation from the pool, based on individual performance, which should be uncapped and decoupled from budget in order to provide the strongest alignment with the interests of shareholders. Best practice in paying out says that there should be a

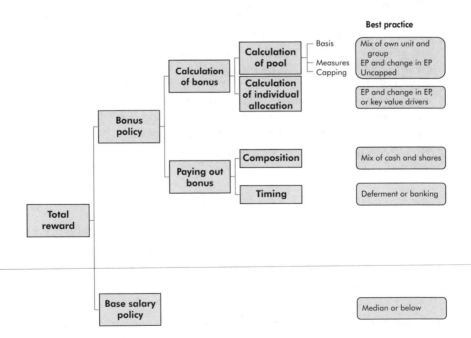

Fig. 23 Best-practice remuneration.

Source: *Managing for Shareholder Value 2002 International Survey Report*, PA Consulting Group.

mixture of cash and shares, which should then be restricted, deferred or banked to ensure a link with long-term performance.

Our research showed that companies that designed performance management and reward systems with these features deliver, on average, a long-term total shareholder return nine percentage points higher per annum than those that do not.

Aligning investor relations

Although this is the least important in terms of its ability to create long-term shareholder value – effective alignment of investor relations adds only (!) seven per cent per annum to long-term total shareholder return – it is nevertheless a big enough impact for CEOs to take very seriously.

There are three elements to aligning investor relations with the creation of long-term shareholder value.

The most obvious is the need to communicate what value has been delivered in the business, for example, by a clear and accurate description of the changes in economic profit, rather than focusing on accounting profit or on earnings per share.

It is also essential to communicate how you run the business in terms of the value-based management processes in place – which actually turns out to make a very great deal of difference to long-term TSR.

Finally, and often overlooked, the CEO must communicate what sort of investors the company wants and what experience they will receive.

This last point sounds a bit bizarre and it is perhaps best illustrated by looking at the example of Warren Buffett, who has actively managed his shareholder base.

First, he explains very clearly how he runs the business (see the Berkshire Hathaway *Owners' Manual*), what he will and will not do in order to push up the share price: he will ensure that he only invests in projects where he believes there is a good return; he will not attempt to talk up the share price or indulge in accounting manoeuvres that do not relate to the fundamental value creation of the business; he will not encourage the share price to rise above what he regards as the intrinsic value of the business, etc. Finally, he encourages investors to buy the Berkshire Hathaway share and hold it for a long time by a variety of means, including not splitting the stock, a deliberate policy to ensure illiquidity of the Berkshire Hathaway shares.

As a result, Berkshire Hathaway has a uniquely loyal and well-informed shareholder base.

There is a serious time-management issue with investor relations: how much effort should the CEO spend preparing and delivering messages for analysts, and how much actually creating value in the business? Most CEOs spend at least two weeks per quarter – around one-sixth of their time – largely with sell-side analysts. This is a serious misallocation: one-sixth is too much and sell-side analysts are the wrong audience.

Ensuring that information flows keep managers grounded in reality

The best-designed processes in the world will be completely ineffective if the managers operating these processes are not firmly grounded in the reality of their business. What can the CEO do to ensure that this is the case? There are three particularly crucial elements that must be in place.

An open channel from customers

There must be an open channel from customers to top management. This can be created in a variety of ways.

UniChem, the UK arm of Alliance UniChem Plc, was originally a co-operative, owned and directed by pharmacists. When it translated to a Plc structure it retained the former regional committees that, in effect, act as institutionalized focus groups. These committees meet quarterly and the members are outspoken in both their praise and their complaints when talking to top management of UniChem. With such a system in place, it is difficult for top management to lose touch with the day-today realities experienced by their customers – and this gives UniChem a significant competitive advantage.

Ben Verwaayen, the CEO of BT, personally answers emails from customers – though of course the resolution of issues raised is rapidly delegated. Again, this keeps him close to the reality of day-to-day customer experiences.

There is no substitute for direct contact with customers.

A finger on the pulse

The CEO should carry out a number of tasks which might seem to be *infra dignitatem*, but which ensure that he or she keeps the finger on the pulse of what is really happening within the business.

Again this is something that can be done in a variety of ways. Most involve getting out of the corner office rather than on relying on management reports to highlight key issues.

When he was Chief Executive at Asda, Archie Norman used to spend his Saturdays carrying out store visits. After each of these visits he would dictate copious notes to be sent to the store managers. This had the twin benefits of keeping him very much aware of the reality on the ground in the business, and of making sure that all his managers were aware that they might be visited at any time and that any shortcomings in the operations of their stores would be highly visible right at the top of the organization.

A second element of keeping a finger on the pulse is the prudence of accounting – another key governance issue. No business can safely run with accounts that are being used principally for support rather than for illumination.

Aligned management information

Management information should be shaped so as to present managers with a true understanding of the economics of their business, in terms that relate to long-term shareholder value, rather than the traditional accounting concepts.

Aligning management information with value creation sounds like the most obvious step for any management to take, and yet our survey showed that only 10–20 per cent of companies make any value-based information available to their managers. Most companies continue to run their businesses on traditional accounting measures.

The importance of giving managers the right information can be seen in the following simple, but realistic, illustration. Imagine a retailer with four main categories of products spread over 4000 square metres of retail space. The four categories have the following characteristics:

Category	Gross profit %	Square metres	Capital cost per sq. m.	Sales per sq. m.	Operating costs as % of sales
A	50%	1,000	2,000	3,000	36%
B	40%	1,000	2,500	4,500	30%
C	47%	1,000	2,000	5,000	45%
D	30%	1,000	1,500	6,000	30%
Total	–	4,000	2,000	4,625	35%

The performance of each category would be as shown below:

Category	Sales per sq. m.	GP per sq. m.	OP per sq. m.	EP per sq. m.
A	3,000	1,500	420	**220**
B	4,500	1,800	**450**	200
C	5,000	**2,350**	100	–100
D	**6,000**	1,800	–	–150
Total	4,625	1,863	243	43

A manager running the business on sales per square metre would naturally increase the space allocation of Category D; a manager who sees GP per square metre would focus on C; a manager who is in the relatively fortunate position of seeing operating profit per square metre would choose B; only the rare manager who sees economic profit per square metre would focus on A, which is where the greatest value potential lies.

Our research showed that, as a result of differences in decision-making like these, companies whose management information was aligned with shareholder value delivered a long-term TSR of more than nine per cent per annum higher than those which did not.

Personally taking the lead role in the most fundamental decisions

Given that effective delegation is one of the keys to success as a CEO, it is important to draw the right boundaries in terms of the decisions in which the CEO should take an active part.

We believe that there are three categories of decision that qualify. These are decisions concerning capital allocation, the ethics or value of the business and the safeguarding of the key capabilities and resources of the firm as described in Chapter 4.

The high-performing CEO: Warren Buffett and Berkshire Hathaway

Warren Buffett is known as the world's most successful investor. Over the four decades since he purchased Berkshire Hathaway in 1964, he has delivered an average total shareholder return of 24 per cent. This is a performance without parallel. But, of course, he is more than just an investor; he is chairman of a diverse group of companies. A cursory glance at the composition of Berkshire Hathaway's portfolio might not reveal the logic behind a textile company that is now involved in everything from candy to reinsurance. The binding logic, which gave rise to the tremendous success of the company, driven by Warren Buffett and his partner Charlie Munger, is not based on the traditional concepts of sector focus or technology capabilities but on an assessment of strategic health and hence intrinsic value.

The billionaire's secret lies in a strict adherence to value-based management and investment. The principles are simple: invest in great businesses (that cannot help but deliver superior returns over time) at fair prices, and withdraw capital from businesses that will not deliver attractive returns. Do not invest in bad business.

In line with these principles, Buffett will only invest in a business if he can be reasonably certain how much it will earn over the next 20–25 years. Such a long-term perspective, driven by a belief in sustainable competitive advantage, is almost unheard of. Of course, the ability to apply these principles requires a number of unusual attributes:

- The ability to recognize such a business in the first place – i.e. to judge when a competitive advantage really is enduring.
- The self-discipline and courage to stick to these principles even when the implications are clearly detrimental in terms of reported accounting profits, short-term impact on market value or simply in terms of being seen to be acting. Professor Higgins, of the University of Washington, attributes Buffett's success to this rigour: 'His secret sauce is incredible discipline. It's one thing to state your purchase strategy or your valuation strategy, and it's quite another to stick to that strategy in bad times as well as good.'
- The financial strength to stick to these principles at times when results are going against you. John Maynard Keynes remarked: 'Markets can remain irrational longer than you can remain solvent.' For almost everyone else, that is true, but not for Warren Buffett, whose decision to eschew debt despite the boost it would give to returns in the short term has given him the ability to exploit enduring market irrationality.

Warren Buffett illustrates how the personal characteristics of the leader shape his company's success. His intelligence, excellent communication skills and strong ethics go some way to explain his fortunes; ultimately, however, it is his drive – despite his describing his own style as 'lethargy bordering on sloth' – and determination that best explain the company's extraordinary performance. An investor who was wise enough, or lucky enough, to put $1,000 into Berkshire Hathaway stock in 1964 would now be sitting on a fortune of over $5 million.

The CEO as capital allocator

No less a CEO than Warren Buffett considers capital allocation decisions as one of the key roles of the CEO. There are three main types of decision for which the CEO must take ultimate responsibility.

Mergers and acquisitions. It is well known that around 70 per cent of all acquisitions destroy shareholder value. Any CEO who wants to be a long-term success must either (and this is the unlikely route) be sure that the approach to acquisitions means that they will fall into the top 30 per cent or (much more likely) create a long-term strategy not based on acquisitions as the fuel for performance.

Investment in existing businesses. In particular, the role of the CEO must be to ensure that the business invests in strategies, not projects. As Warren Buffett says: 'We rarely invest significant amounts of capital to turn around the performance of poor businesses.' It makes sense to approve capital expenditure far more readily for a business whose strategy should be to grow (because it creates shareholder value at the moment and can be expected to do so in the future) than for one whose strategy should be to shrink to a profitable core.

Dividends and share buy-backs. There are two reasons for doing a share buy-back, one good and the other bad. The good reason is in a situation where the shares are seriously undervalued so that they can be bought in the market for significantly less than their discounted cash-flow value. The result is that the business creates long-term shareholder value by buying back its shares.

The bad reason is for share buy-back motivated by the knowledge that short-term market forces will cause any share to rise temporarily if it is bought in large quantities.

In the last three or four years, many good businesses have been damaged, some irrevocably (for example, Marconi), by poor capital allocation. The whole telecoms sector has been gravely wounded by poor capital allocation. A single large misallocation of capital can undo a decade's worth of careful management.

How not to allocate capital: the 3G licence story

The purchase of 3G licences in the telecommunications industry is a classic example of capital misallocation – and one that would have been avoided if companies had had strong management processes in place.

Here are the facts:

- Total mobile phone subscribers in the UK, Germany, France: 140 million, representing around 70 per cent of the population of those countries.
- Average revenue per user (ARPU) on existing phone services: €423; average operating profit margin on these sales: five per cent.
- Total investment in 3G licences: €102 billion; investment in network at €525/subscriber: €72 billion.
- Earnings needed to provide a return on total investment above: €16 billion. Operating profit implied (assuming no debt): €22 billion.

To believe that they would get a return, then, the bidders must have assumed either:

- That future operating profit margin on these sales would be around 39 per cent (vs the 5 per cent historic figure)
- That future ARPU would be around €3,100 (against €423 historically)
- Or some combination of the two.

It is difficult not to assume, considering the facts (and at least some telcos were provided these facts at the time they made these decisions), that the companies in question decided to buy a licence at any cost, ignoring any management processes that may have been in place in their organizations. With strong decision processes in place, they would have walked away – and bought up over-paying competitors at bargain prices after the inevitable crash.

Decisions which change the ethics or values of the business

We have seen in the recent disasters at Enron and many other companies how strong the impact of corporate ethos is on personal ethics; and how devastating the loss of personal ethics is for corporate performance. The behaviours, actions and decisions of the top managers of any organization carry disproportionate weight and the CEO, in particular, has a great personal impact on the ethics of the organization he or she runs.

This point relates as much to leadership, perhaps more, as it does to management, but the example of Enron shows how management processes and reward systems can encourage behaviour that becomes unethical. The CEO should check that the management processes in place will not tend to push people in the direction of unethical behaviour in order to hit performance targets.

In summary

While strong management alone cannot ensure the success of a business, weak management can certainly sink it.

The role of the CEO as a manager is to control the overall direction of decision-making, without attempting to take every decision personally.

This means striking a careful but difficult balance. To help achieve this balance the CEO must:

- Allow for decision delegation by creating a team of people whose decision-making the CEO is comfortable to rely on

- Shape the key management decision-making processes explicitly to guide the decisions of this team and others in line with maximizing shareholder value

- Not get too far from the business. Create information flows that keep all managers grounded in the reality of the business

- Above all, show the way where it matters most. Take the lead role, personally, in the most fundamental decisions facing the organization.

Only then will the CEO be able to create the right dynamic between personal decision-making and delegation.

7 An organization that knows itself

You have the strategy clear now. It is robust and articulates a winning business model that you are sure you can deliver. You have identified the capabilities and resources necessary to build and sustain this model. The potential for growth and returns from implementing the model both look great. You have run the numbers and are set to create tremendous long-term shareholder value. On the face of it you are ready to create a high-performance organization.

Unfortunately you can't do it on your own: you may need 150,000 people to help you deliver this vision. Unless they understand the vision and sign up to it, you won't make progress; unless they stay signed up, the model will never materialize as a reality. What makes it more complicated is that you don't even know most of these people.

Many CEOs make the assumption that their people understand what the business is trying to achieve, agree with the direction, care about it and act accordingly.

Where the assumption is valid, the organization has the potential to achieve great things; where it is not, poor performance is the likely outcome.

The impact of a CEO who is effective as both a leader and manager is manifest in an organization that knows itself.

Mission statements are not enough

We encounter good intentions in a multitude of strategic frameworks: missions and visions, multiple lists of so-called values, dense strategy documents and operational plans, brand identities, customer propositions and advertising straplines.

It is difficult to convert this complexity into effective action. The number and inconsistency, the often condescending language and top-down style of such frameworks can obscure the focus on what really matters, preventing individuals from understanding their personal role and contribution, alienating rather than engaging them.

Mission statements are usually predictable: 'our mission is to maximize value to our shareholders by providing total quality services, empowering customer-oriented employees and growing through new markets and technologies.'

As well as being bland, idealistic inventions of uninspired committees, missions are usually supported by other statements – such as visions, strategies and brands – without a clear understanding of their role or how they fit together.

When it comes to organizational values, these are similarly a list of admirable hygiene factors for any business today: 'customers, innovation, respect, collaborative, efficient, secure.'

Organizational values often coexist alongside lists of brand values and various lists of functional axioms. In most companies, they are impossible for employees to remember – let alone derive any inspiration or guidance from.

So how *do* you bring people together with a clear and compelling agenda?

What is required to achieve focus across the business on the activities and markets, the capabilities and actions that matter most? How can you engage a large and diverse workforce? And make a corporate objective personally relevant to each person so that they will do their job better?

The simple answer would be to say 'communication'. And that is 50 per cent correct. However, defining one-dimensional lines and lists of words, and seeking to dictate them to the rest of the organization, is unlikely to create commitment, belief and energy. A second complication is in distilling the right messages. As we discussed earlier, shareholder value is delivered through a winning business model. Without this, you cannot hope to succeed. You therefore need your people to understand this model and to manage it so that it does create the promised value. We also discussed the problem for any business model of built-in obsolescence: as soon it starts to become clear that it is successful, it spawns imitators and these imitators themselves reduce the effectiveness of the model. You therefore need to keep refining the model; you need your people to understand it – but not become so wedded to it that they cannot change to embrace the competitive and market challenges to which the business will be forever exposed.

In professional services businesses, for example, there are often themes that dictate that a certain area of business will be larger or more profitable than another over the next year or so. Examples towards the end of the last millennium were e-business and Y2K. Any business which made a large irreversible commitment of resources in these directions, however, would have suffered badly or even gone out of business after the turn of the millennium (and some did).

The building blocks of the business are much more likely to endure. For example, in the luxury goods business, brand will always be the key. In professional services businesses, being able to recruit and develop the best people will always be a source of potential competitive advantage.

This gives, in effect, two very different layers of message – the **urgent**, which relates to how money is being made now and to which people must respond with alacrity, and the **important**, which relates to issues that will remain true despite the fluctuations in the market or the short-term behaviour of competitors and which should guide the deeper and more far-reaching decisions taken by the organization.

In short, the CEO has two key challenges:

• How to think about the message you want to communicate

- How to manage the practicalities of communicating that content effectively.

What is the message you want to communicate?

The substance of the message must reflect the business model that the organization is operating now, as well as the capabilities and resources that it is preserving in order to rebuild and refresh that model. To communicate the key points about these things effectively, successful CEOs create messages that relate to purpose, personality and performance (see Figure 24). We set out below some of the ways in which they do this.

- **Purpose** … to define the direction … and make it real.

- **Personality** … to build a distinctive character … and bring it to life.

- **Performance** … to relate it to today … and make it work.

An organization that really knows itself has an intuitive sense of direction and what is right, enabling focus and alignment across the business. It has people who can explain its purpose and strategy concisely in their own words, with belief and conviction. As well as this, there is a distinctive character that makes the organization stand out from others and is compelling to employees and customers. To make it happen requires the internal energy to turn promises into reality, to pursue and continually achieve high performance.

Fig. 24 Communicating key points.

Such organizations have confidence and walk tall. They are focused and persistent, and dedicated to their purpose. They may sometimes appear arrogant or inflexible, but that is more a reflection of their confidence, and the lack of it in others. (As we have repeatedly stated, companies that genuinely suffer from arrogance and inflexibility are, of course, in danger.) They know what they are doing, and believe in it, and are at ease with themselves. There are three sets of challenges for a CEO in building such a company. These are:

Purpose, to define the business direction, and create desire to achieve it

- *Strategy:* setting out clearly where the organization is going, explaining how this will create value, defining priorities and retaining flexibility.

- *Mission:* defining the business's role in the market and its mission as a business, creating a unique reason for being.

- *Vision:* building a collective understanding of what the business will look like and feel like in the future and what it means in the context of today's actions.

Personality, to build a distinctive character, and bring it to life

- *Beliefs:* the core principles and actions that exist throughout the business, required to achieve the distinctive purpose.

- *Brand:* articulating the core purpose in a way that is clear and compelling to all audiences using a wide range of symbols.

- *Engagement:* building confidence in people, the conviction and belief that the ambition is worthy and achievable, and generating from them the behaviours that are essential to achieve it.

Performance, to relate the purpose to today, and make it work

- *Focus:* bringing focus to the strategic priorities, understanding what matters most from resource allocation to delivered results.

- *Energy:* building and sustaining organization momentum, which gives people the adrenalin to perform and raise their game.

- *Behaviour:* making everyday actions intuitive, while also seeing today's decisions and activities in the context of the broader purpose.

While this might sound like a daunting agenda, the good news is that much of what is needed already exists in your organization today. By design or default the organization will have adopted some form of mission, some distinctive ways of working, and cultural priorities.

The bad news is that history or circumstance may well have delivered the wrong answers. They are likely to be fragmented and, quite probably, inconsistent with, maybe opposite to, your strategic aspirations.

An organization that knows itself must be built on what exists. It must be founded on the business model and the building blocks already identified by the CEO (see Figure 25).

It is not a blue-sky exercise. While the ambition may well be a new one, most of the ways of achieving it will need to evolve from the realities of today. This will provide unique challenges and opportunities for every organization.

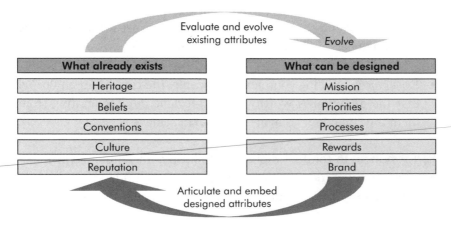

Fig. 25 Building an organization that knows itself.
Source: PA analysis.

The CEO's role in creating an organization with 'purpose'

PURPOSE	CEO responsibility	Organization benefit
Distil the **strategy essence**	A rigorous but practical strategy defining how value is created	A clear understanding of what we are seeking to achieve and why
Define a stretching **mission**	A stretching and compelling mission for the business	A clear understanding of what we need to do to get there
Crystallize the **vision**	Articulating the mission and strategy in a tangible way	Ability to relate day-to-day activities to the future direction

Many businesses can be misled, in the attempt to address purpose, by the temptation to ignore reality and set a mission unrelated to the potential for value creation. If they succeed in developing or implementing a strategy to achieve this mission, they will still have no guarantee of high performance.

High-performing organizations do it differently. They confront reality, however brutal, *before* determining a value-creating strategy. From this strategy they distil mission (not the other way around), which will act as a powerful motivating force for managers and staff, and they make it practical by crystallizing a vision as a step along the way (see Figure 26).

Strategy essence: What are we going to do?

The basis for creation of a motivating ambition is a clear strategy, which explains how the business will create value for stakeholders. Earlier, we explored the ingredients of a good strategy, one that clearly defines where the company will play, how it will compete and how it will be profitable. This should provide the basis of the content of the message. There is a danger, however: strategy documents are notoriously long

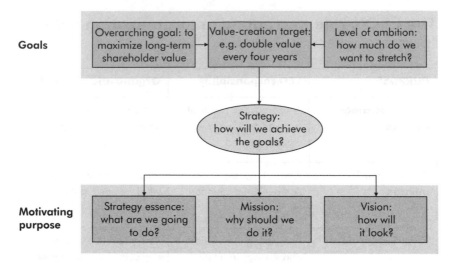

Fig. 26 The what, why and how.
Source: PA analysis.

and boring; therefore, they can easily be intimidating to their readers – that is if they are ever read.

The basic problem in communicating strategy is that it is often created without the engagement of the people who must drive and deliver it; typically framed in language that is neither memorable nor inspiring, aimed at finance and strategy people; and in the worst cases, lacking bite once it has been through various committees and rewrites.

A *good* strategy is therefore one that is rigorous and definitive, practical and engaging. It must be right, but it must also be compelling in its *articulation* if people are to understand and remember it, act on and be energized by it.

The strategy at FedEx brings focus to its business, by stating it is 'dedicated to maximizing financial returns by providing a totally reliable, competitively superior, global air-ground transportation of high-priority goods and documents that require rapid, time-certain delivery'. This short paragraph defines the essence of the business model and the scope of its applicability.

While this is clearly a short form of the strategy of FedEx, it does help to capture the essence. Strategies seek opportunities to upset industry equilibrium, allow a business to disrupt the 'normal' course of industry events and to forge new industry conditions for sustained competitive advantage.

Mission: Why should we do it?

The organization's purpose should be distilled into a compelling mission, which explains the business's unique reason for being. It usually defines this in terms of its added value to customers, rather than employees or shareholders because, without a clear position within a marketplace, there is no opportunity to create the value exchange that sits at the heart of any business.

The mission should describe what the business sets out to do uniquely for customers. A compelling ambition should generally therefore focus on the high-level benefit that the company seeks to deliver to customers over time. How will it add value to people's lives? Or even, what is its role in society? Although it might not be achievable at once, it is a cause that the organization is committed to fighting for.

A traditional mission statement, in comparison, tends to mix up the goals of the business for investors with its role for customers, and so loses focus on the latter. A *vision* statement tends to support a mission statement, by describing what it will feel like when the mission is accomplished: 'Imagine a world where ...'

The retail giant Wal-Mart's mission is to 'reduce the cost of living for everyone everywhere', which is indeed a noble purpose, which is likely to motivate its 1.2 million partners to turn up for work with a passion each day, as well as being attractive to customers.

Microsoft's mission is 'to unleash the creativity in every person, every family, and every business. Because we believe the real measure of success is not the power of our software but the power it unleashes in you.'

Vision: How will it look?

The third aspect of purpose is perhaps the most important in that it enables action – in the context of working towards the mission, guided by the more practical strategy. Effective communication of this mission and strategy builds a collective understanding and approach.

Prêt à Manger's vision is brought to life by a 'passion for food'. A diverse and transient workforce is brought together by a common passion for the very best ingredients within their sandwiches, cakes and coffee. This passion is infectious between their people, and with customers.

At Virgin, the vision is brought to life by a collective desire to challenge conventions, to stand up for the consumer and take on the dominant force of market leaders. There is only one initial reason why Virgin will enter a new market, 'because we can change things'.

The CEO's role in creating an organization with 'personality'

PERSONALITY	CEO responsibility	Organization benefit
Define the core **beliefs**	Common set of beliefs – values, attitudes, conventions	We understand what is the desired and acceptable as a way of working
Develop a strong **brand**	Articulating the core purpose and competitive advantage	We have a common identity which captures our difference
Deploy to gain **engagement**	Bringing this character to life collectively and for each individual	We are engaged as individuals and as a team across the business

Beliefs: What do we really believe in?

At the core of anyone's personality are the values, principles and motivations that guide and drive them. These 'beliefs', conscious and unconscious, provide a consistent anchor and a framework around which we form ambitions and opinions, the way in which we think and behave.

The same is true in organizations. Compare the sales-driven culture of a company like Compaq, where the focus is on selling as many boxes as possible, to the more esoteric culture of a fashion brand like Armani, or the intellectually rigorous culture of a management consultancy.

At innovators 3M, there is fundamental belief in innovation, a symbol of which is the time every person is encouraged to spend 'bootlegging'. Nike's fundamental belief is in sporting excellence, building its global headquarters as a sports complex, with a driveway lined with statues of its sporting greats, and a fitness centre at the heart of the campus.

However, not all organizations use their beliefs to their advantage. This entails recognizing beliefs as more than the conventions by which business happens, the underlying motivations of direction and focus; using them as a source of business alignment and competitive advantage, a foundation on which to build the business; ensuring that they exist at both rational and emotional levels, rational because they are practical, emotional because they are engaging; and aligning individual beliefs with collective beliefs, ensuring that people are in tune with each other, and the business has a common agenda.

Beliefs are not to be taken lightly. Bill Bernbach, co-founder of Doyle Dane Bernbach, made the much-quoted comment: 'a principle is not a principle unless it costs you money'. Before signing up to a long list of well-intentioned 'beliefs', or making others sign up to them, the CEO should check that he or she is prepared to act on them even if they cost money. For this reason, we suggest limiting the formal 'beliefs' of the company to ethical issues.

In particular, it always makes sense to have a principle of truthful reporting of performance (even if that might mean missing a quarter's earnings numbers). Equally, although it is admirable to have a strong preference for no redundancies, it might not always make practical sense to elevate it into a principle.

Brand: What makes us special?

The corporate brand *articulates* the purpose and personality of the organization in a distinctive, memorable and engaging way – for customers.

However, this is a very limited way to think of corporate brands. Brands are as much for employees and shareholders as they are for customers; they can be communicated in many forms, much more than a logo; and at a corporate level they should fit with other brands in the business.

Indeed, brands exist in many states – an idea and promise, a name and logo, an experience and reputation. Brands are functional, comparative and emotional. Functionally the brand is about the core attributes of the product or service, Coca-Cola is about refreshment or Honda is about engines. Comparatively, the brand is about its differences: Volvo is safer or Dell is more customized. Emotionally, the brand is what it does for you: Nike gives you attitude or Virgin is on your side.

The CEO's challenge is to ensure the brands connect with the desired purpose of the business; to align the business so that the brands work internally and externally to be the brand champion, spokesperson and guardian.

The corporate brand brings to life the personality of the brand; it is shorthand for everything the business is about and seeking to achieve; it is among the most useful leadership tools that the CEO has.

Engagement: Inspiring confidence

Personality only works if it lives inside the people who make up the business – building confidence, the conviction and belief that the ambition is worthy and achievable, and bringing a motivation and style to the business which drives it to deliver the ambition short and longer term.

The character is communicated through words and symbols, gestures and behaviours that are memorable and meaningful to each audience.

Microsoft has used a cartoon character call 'Mickey Soft' as part of its internal communication, as a way to articulate what it believes in, and how it works. This is fun, engaging and memorable. By building a character that people get to know, if they need inspiration as to how to behave they can say, 'What would Mickey do?'

Hewlett Packard has turned to the increasingly popular technique of storytelling to get its message across to both employees and customers. It has recreated the 'legend' of its founders, how Hewlett and Packard jammed together in their California garage, inventing their initial computer prototypes. HP's objective was to instil the spirit of 'invention' back into their business in a way that is more than a strapline or list of values.

The complete CEO: Howard Schultz at Starbucks

Howard Schultz believes passionately in the community. This belief has fuelled the growth of one of the most instantly recognizable brands in the world to a billion-dollar business – without recourse to traditional mass-marketing methods.

The Starbucks experience is more than just a great cup of coffee – when Schultz started out he also wanted to build 'a company with soul'. This ranged from making sure all employees working over 20 hours per week got healthcare cover to ensuring that a fair price was paid to coffee growers. Living his passion and vision has produced an organization that extends to over 35 countries and 9,000 stores but has still managed to retain the feeling of a small, community meeting place within its stores. The company constantly endeavours to increase this feeling associated with entering a Starbucks, bringing in Wi-Fi, music and seating arrangements that enable cosy gatherings of friends.

Unlike many other global brands, Schultz has always been insistent that the company owns the majority of Starbucks stores rather than franchise as he feels it is only possible to standardize the brand identity and values with this approach. The challenge has been to 'stay small' and remain nimble and entrepreneurial while operating on such a global scale. His answer has been to allow the individual stores to develop their own place in the community, building a bond with the individual customer, while adhering to the company-wide balance between profitability and social consciousness.

Schultz's approach to business, making Starbucks 'a people business serving coffee' rather than just another coffee store, provides a sound base for the cornerstone of the Starbucks brand: that of the association with a product it can rely on to represent a system of values and ethics that stand out against the increasingly cynical consumer environment.

Despite this insistence on core values, however, Schultz is willing to take risks if it will enhance the Starbucks brand, or if it will benefit the local community. In a recent reversal of previous policy, stores in Seattle now stock doughnuts produced by a local manufacturer. The experiment was a resounding success, building on an initial word-of-mouth 'buzz' in the city to increase the success of a local company and also increase local coffee sales as more people visited the stores. In addition, he is extremely proactive in the introduction of new ideas, using the direct contact with customers to road test a number of ideas per year.

Although Schultz is still expanding Starbucks, he is adamant that the only way for this to happen is to preserve the core while extending the experience. As he said, in business, 'compromise everything but your core values'. This stance has also proved popular with shareholders: annualized TSR for the period 1994–2004 is an impressive 34 per cent.

The CEO's role in creating an organization with 'performance'

PERFORMANCE	CEO responsibility	Organization benefit
Define a clear **focus**	Focus on the strategic priorities for the short and long term	We know what we need to do, and why it matters
Develop high **energy**	Building organization momentum and adrenalin to perform	We are ready and willing to put everything into it
Deploy the right **behaviour**	Delivering the right actions today which will also create tomorrow	I know that I am making a vital contribution to our success

The CEO's best trick in creating an organization that really knows itself is to manage the balance between creating the future and delivering today – to start making the mission happen in practical actions day by day.

Focus: What are the business priorities?

This is about bringing context and focus to the many activities that everybody across the business is working on.

- *Context is provided by the purpose and personality that are designed to create the organization*

- *Focus is provided by understanding the areas and actions that matter most to the business, and to customers.*

Business focus is ultimately about making the decisions that fit with the long term, and taking the actions that have most impact on performance. Customer focus is about understanding the most important needs of target customers, and delivering them in a relevant and competitively superior way.

Energy: Are we up for doing it?

This is about building momentum in the business – ensuring that intent has a bias to action – and that the 'potential energy' of the business is mobilized into 'kinetic energy'. The scientific analogy is an appropriate one because once the inertia is overcome, which typically exists when getting new things started, it is then much easier to progress. The challenge is often therefore to get started – requiring additional effort and catalysts.

For example, Nike's sales team are known as 'Ekins', i.e. Nike spelt backwards. They are the ultimate ambassadors – and enthusiasts – for their brand. Their belief and dedication is infectious within their team, and hopefully with the retailers who they seek to stock and sell their merchandise. Indeed, many Ekins even have the swoosh tattooed on their ankles.

Energy must be both individual and collective. Each person must be energized to make a difference, to push boundaries, and deliver their part of the jigsaw. However, organization energy is a much more powerful force, combining the drive of individuals to make significant progress and change happen.

Behaviour: Are we doing it?

This is about making everyday actions intuitive, while also seeing today's decisions and activities in the context of the broader purpose.

One of the most inspirational leaders of recent times has been Herb Kelleher at Southwest Airlines – the airline which created the low-cost, short-haul model, but also went on to redefine levels of customer service while keeping prices low. The Harley Davidson-driving CEO creates a personality for the business that is translated into performance through the everyday actions of his people. It is up to staff to choose the most appropriate way to serve – and entertain – their passengers on each flight.

Kelleher, the fun-loving CEO, would think nothing of hiding in an over-head locker and jumping out to surprise passengers as they board the plane. Therefore, if cabin crew feel bored on a mid-afternoon flight, and customers look as though they need cheering up, then announcing an impromptu competition with champagne to the winners is quite in line with the business purpose and personality. Not only this, but Southwest is an excellent example of how a distinctive style can deliver superior financial performance too.

What are the practicalities of getting the message across?

This is all very well but ultimately there is still the task of getting 150,000 (or however many people it is) to understand. So how do you do this? The answer is to use leadership and management tools to create hard and soft messages to all parts of the organization.

The John Lewis Partnership (JLP) in the UK is an example of an organization whose success may be largely down to the fact that it knows itself – and that it is able to convey the appropriate messages to its staff. From the customer viewpoint JLP delivers high-quality products at a fair price and with genuinely customer-focused service: JLP staff will give good, unbiased advice to customers even if that means sacrificing a sale in the short term. Although the concepts are simple, getting the alignment needed to deliver this has proven extremely difficult for others to replicate, and JLP's competitive advantage has proven enduring. The problem for competitors is that the roots of these behaviours run very deep – reflecting the ownership and reward structures of the business (as well as more easily copied issues like training and performance measurement) – and are very hard to replicate.

Figure 27 illustrates some of the most important signals or message carriers that influence the behaviour of an individual member of a large organization and whose misalignment makes it impossible to create an organization that knows itself.

Hard messages are typically those with numbers in personal objectives, direct instructions from the boss, key performance indicators (KPIs) and the output of the management information system (MIS). It is good management that ensures that these messages are indeed sending the right signals.

The soft messages are often more subtle, but no less important. Examples include symbolic actions taken by the leadership of the business or indeed by the direct boss of the individual; simple leading by example; the corporate values (those which are demonstrably held as values rather than the long list which many organizations have written down but often appear to honour more in the breach than the observance); the

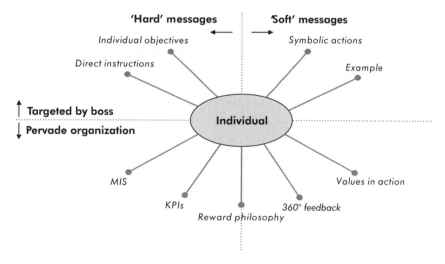

Fig. 27 Message carriers as seen by an individual in the organization.

messages contained in 360-degree feedback. Sitting somewhere on the border is the corporate reward philosophy: this is clearly hard in the sense that it represents numbers, indeed money, but it is also deeply symbolic of what the organization really values from each individual. Good leadership is required to keep these messages aligned.

Looking at this picture, we can see immediately that some of the message carriers are like carving in stone while others more resemble writing on paper. For example, embedding economic profits throughout the organization is a major undertaking that takes years and, indeed, would take years to reverse. At the other end of the spectrum, changing somebody's objectives is something that happens naturally every year: targeting a different market in 2008 from that which was focused on in 2007 is very straightforward. This difference implies that some of the message carriers are better directed at measuring the transient while others are powerful ways of reminding people of the permanent.

Ensuring congruence between the hard and the soft side is absolutely critical: if you don't really believe in the messages yourself, inevitably, your leadership will undermine your management.

It is also clear that many of these messages are delivered either consciously or unconsciously by the individual's boss, or boss's boss. This implies that you cannot create this kind of alignment bottom-up; it has to be a top-down process.

Cascading until you have an organization that knows itself

Now the messages have to cascade from the top down until they have created an organization that knows itself.

The cascading process actually has to start with the CEO and with the top team. They should explicitly check that they are both leading and managing themselves in a way that is appropriate to the organization they are trying to build. Paradoxically, changing the 'hard' elements like personal objectives, measures and rewards turns out to be much easier than changing the 'soft' elements such as symbolic actions. Only when you are sure that you have it right at the top level should you begin the cascade, because only then can you be sure that you will be credible to the next level down.

The next step is to design the cascade. Clearly if there are 150,000 people in the organization, you cannot design the messages individually, but you can divide the organization into groups, each of which will be addressed in roughly the same way, and leave the details of individual performance objectives to be set by managers, trusting that because they themselves understand the messages, they will do so appropriately.

Finally, you need to roll it out. This is a never-ending process. First, of course, there is the problem of cascading down through the organization until all staff have been reached. And this, of course, is complicated by the fact that some of the messages – the transient parts – will change during this process. But then there is the problem that in an organization of 150,000 people with ten per cent turnover, for example, 15,000 new people need to absorb the message, understand it and become committed to it every year. You need sustaining mechanisms to make sure that the organization continues to know itself.

An interesting example is used by PA Consulting Group. Ernest Butten, a powerful and principled leader who created one of the most success-ful consulting firms in the world, founded PA. When he retired in 1970, Butten made a video setting out what he believed were the fundamental principles that underpin the success of PA. As part of the induction process, all new recruits are shown this video in which Ernest Butten sets out the importance of recruiting the very best people and of focusing hard on clients. The business model of PA has changed beyond all recognition since Butten left but those building blocks remain the same, and Ernest Butten still helps to make the firm an organization that knows itself.

In summary

Sustaining high performance over many years requires the ability to get a large number of people to focus simultaneously on being agile in reacting to current market threats and opportunities while at the same time stubbornly protecting those things that are the building blocks of future success. To do this requires a determined, systematic and sustained approach to creating an organization in which all the employees truly understand what is urgent and what is important.

The high-performing CEO: Robert Tillman and Lowe

Robert Tillman rose up the ranks at Lowe, from store manager to CEO, transforming the company from a regional operator to America's number two home-improvement chain. Launching a fierce battle with Home Depot, Tillman faced a retail giant determined to tackle any competitor head-on.

In response, Tillman launched a strategy that focused on the number one's weakest spot – women. Such a strategy exemplified a remarkable insight into the workings behind the DIY market, with women driving decisions behind many purchases. Tillman's market understanding enabled Lowe to position itself competitively against archrival Home Depot, which focused on the traditional male customer and dismissed woman as light DIY-ers with low profit margins. In contrast, Tillman realized that 'once you build loyalty with women, you can hit a home run'.

Moving away from a highly aggressive pricing policy in the style of its Goliath rival, Tillman executed a growth strategy focused on sustaining low prices and excellent customer service. His origins on the shop floor manifested themselves through a focus on the consumer's shopping experience. Not only were outlets redesigned to create a lighter, cleaner and brighter atmosphere, but he also installed customer call buttons on each aisle. However, below its pleasant exterior, Tillman built muscle in the form of one of the best inventory systems in the industry and a 'store-per-door' distribution system that minimized freight costs experienced by smaller loads.

During Tillman's tenure, Lowe expanded its retail chain from 375 to 1075 outlets and grew sales from $7.5 billion in 1994 to $30.8 billion in 2003. Such achievements are even more impressive when contrasted with those of Home Depot, whose shares declined by 40 per cent between 2001 and 2003, compared to an 80 per cent increase for Lowe. The ten-year annualized TSR from 1994 to 2004 was 21 per cent.

Kenneth Lewis, Chairman, CEO and President of the Bank of America commented: 'Bob Tillman's 42 years of experience at Lowe's represent one of the great success stories in American business' (March 2005).

Part 3

The CEO's Challenges

Almost every CEO will encounter the following issues as they take up, exercise and relinquish the role:

- Section 1: Negotiating the contract – seize the opportunity to use your own package as a lever for performance

- Section 2: Managing the first 100 days – build the foundations of your future success

- Section 3: Dealing with underperforming businesses – intervene fast, but in the most constructive ways

- Section 4: Dealing with underperforming individuals – understand the difference at the top level

- Section 5: Making mergers and acquisitions – don't be part of the 80 per cent who destroy value

- Section 6: Dealing with investors – make your communications appeal to long-term investors, not traders

- Section 7: Knowing when and how to go.

For each of these issues, Part 3 sets out some fundamental (but easily forgotten) considerations to take into account.

1 Negotiating the contract

Congratulations, you have got the job of CEO. However, before you crack open the champagne you still have a few loose ends to clear up. In particular, your contract.

The world has a pretty poor view of CEOs thanks, in large part, to their pay schemes, the huge numbers of options that are exercised, the shares sold and the cash banked immediately before a slump in the share price. A failed CEO walks away from the company with a multimillion dollar settlement while the people on the shop floor walk away with two weeks' money and the address of the local employment office. A recent survey put CEOs of corporations lower down the popularity scale than politicians and just above used-car salesmen. If you don't want to be that kind of CEO, you need to pay attention to the way your contract looks.

As CEO-to-be, you should approach your contract from the viewpoint of maximizing the chances of long-term success.

The managing for shareholder value research we carried out demonstrates that there is a premium for aligning managers' remuneration with the creation of long-term shareholder value. In Part 2 of this book we discussed the importance of symbolic action in leadership. It therefore follows that you should lead from the front by adopting a totally aligned contract.

The remuneration package

There are five main components of your package to consider: joining, basic pay, bonus, pension and termination arrangements.

Joining

The key to alignment is personal ownership. So get some shares – straight shares, not options. A survey by US-based consulting firm Clark/Bardes concluded that the correlation between executives with stock and company success is as high as 54 per cent. At the same time, the correlation for options owners was inverse. Something in the region of two or three times salary seems about right. The CEO should have to hang on to the shares for at least five years.

Basic pay

As we have said many times in this book, leadership is symbolic action. In most countries the CEO's salary is public knowledge. As CEO, what do you want observers to think? You should ask for a moderate basic salary, as the upside should come with the bonus. In most countries, what causes bad publicity is pay for failure – pay for success is seen as reasonable.

Bonus

This is where the real money is earned. What you want is a bonus that has no limit and is tied directly to the long-term generation of economic profit (EP). Clearly, historical EPs should be taken into account, but a direct percentage of EP generated should be reasonable. However, EP is still an accounting figure that can be messed about with, so the shareholders will want to see that a significant proportion of EP-measured gains, say 50 per cent, is paid in shares, real shares, that the CEO must hold on to for five years before selling, and that some form of bonus banking arrangement is in place so that losses can be subtracted from profits. If the firm loses money, why not the CEO?

By accepting shares as part of the bonus, the CEO should begin to build a sizeable holding in the firm. Many successful CEOs have a sizeable amount of their wealth tied up in the company they run.

Pension

Many people were appalled at the pension given to Jack Welch on leaving General Electric, some $700,000 a month. This is clearly not the kind of impression you want to create. In a perfect world the CEO would only take a standard company pension – usually a direct percentage of your salary per month (and the same percentage as everyone else in the company). It is your job to build that perfect world so your future wealth should be the same as all the other pensioners in the world – tied to the shareholder value you deliver.

Termination

Not all contracts run smoothly. What if you fall out with the chairman, or active investors revolt, or some other disaster occurs that means that your contract will be terminated? It can happen to the best CEOs. Ideally, your contract should protect you. But if you want to be employed again, the dignity with which you leave and the sanity of your termination package will come into play. One year's salary is enough, together with an ability to keep the shares you have. (Hopefully the CEO that follows will deliver shareholder value.)

The high-performing CEO: Richard Schulze and Best Buy

It is increasingly unusual in the business community for one person to have founded and nurtured a company from a single store to over 700. This, however, is precisely what has happened to Best Buy Co., the largest specialist electronics and home entertainment retailers in the USA. From one shop in St. Paul's, Minnesota, Best Buy now extends across the continental USA and also has stores in Hawaii and Canada.

In 1966, Richard Schulze founded the first store in the Best Buy chain, then known as 'Sound of Music'. Within four years of trading, annual revenue passed the $1 million mark: a phenomenal rate of growth, but one that has been matched regularly throughout the chain's history. Schulze's awareness of technological advances has enabled Best Buy to stock and support new technologies as they have become available, allowing the continued expansion of the number of lines sold. In addition, rapid adaptation to changing conditions meant that the stores could continue to profit even in the face of adversity: Best Buy's 'tornado sales' of the 1980s – selling off products at a discounted price in a 'no frills' environment – came about after a store was literally hit by a tornado. This initiative proved so successful that it became an annual Sound of Music event.

Best Buy's continued success is, in large part, due to Schulze's willingness to change and adapt to customer requirements. When he realized a commission-based pay structure adversely affected relationships with customers, it was replaced with a bonus scheme based around departmental profits. When the opportunity arose to streamline operations by restructuring to aggregate resources, Schulze was quick to make the necessary changes. Inventory turns improved throughout the late 1990s, reaching over seven rotations by 2000.

Currently, the company is rolling out its customer-centric shopping concept across the chain, providing a more specialized service for different consumer sub-populations. This includes an expanded provision for post-sales care, with the 'Geek Squad' (electronics after-sales team) having a presence in every store, and a targeted repair turnaround time of seven days. The expansion of the number of 'stores within a store' in the chain, designed to appeal to additional market sub-sectors, also allows customers with a particular requirement to discuss their needs with a specialist supplier. Such a focused approach means that customers are able to build up personal relationships with the sales team on the shop floor.

Schulze is quick to delegate management problems to his senior management team, acknowledging that 'There isn't one mind smart enough to have all the answers.' He believes the company's success is in large part due to the unique culture in the company, which creates a shopping experience that customers keep coming back to.

The combination of the effects resulted in shareholders benefiting from an annualized TSR of 28 per cent for the period 1994–2004.

2 Managing the first 100 days

You are now the CEO of a significant business. Your new responsibilities are huge and complex. If you have been promoted from within, you know the company – it is the job that is different; if brought in from the outside, although you may have been a CEO before, you will find this company is different. In either case, the job is challenging and the stakes are high.

How can you ensure that you will be successful? Make sure that you use your first 100 days to build the foundations of your future success – there are things you can do in this period more easily than at any other time during your tenure:

- Understanding the issues

- Strengthening your team

- Setting the direction for the business.

In general, this is all you need to do, but in some cases the business situation may demand rapid action, to fix liquidity or performance problems, for example.

Ben Verwaayen and the first 100 days at BT

When he became CEO of BT in January 2002, Ben Verwaayen had clear priorities: 'Set the tone, get the right people in place and set the agenda for the future'.

Verwaayen was acutely conscious of the impact of inadvertent signalling during the first 100 days: 'You have to realize that you instantly change the pecking order, just by spending time talking to A rather than B. You must be careful to include all those you want in the team.' He was nevertheless in favour of making one or two decisive moves quickly – and then creating stability among the management team.

Verwaayen spent 80 per cent of his time communicating (though this was only possible because he knew the business so well before joining, he says). 'People must hear you talk, or myths start spreading,' he explains. He insisted on talking about 'us' rather than 'you' even in his first few days in order to demonstrate that he was now on board and in charge. He was quick to remove many of the signs of executive superiority that he found on joining BT (such as an 'executive lift'). Setting the tone, in other words, was a priority.

The most difficult item on the list, says Verwaayen, is setting the agenda – particularly if you are new to the sector. In the case of BT, he was helped by two factors: that he knew the industry well; and that BT was in a state where it was clear that certain fire-fighting actions were required.

On this basis, Verwaayen felt confident enough to speak to analysts about the way forward after only four weeks in the job.

Understanding the issues

In the first few days of your appointment you have a licence to ask those within the business – at all levels – and a range of external stakeholders, some truly fundamental questions about the business. This gives you an ability to find out what people really think of the business in a way that can become far more difficult over time. This puts the new CEO in a better position than anyone else to form a balanced judgement of the issues facing the business. And this judgement is, of course, critical to being able to set the direction for the business.

In the early days, more CEOs are fired because of interpersonal than perform-ance issues; it is important, therefore, not to underestimate their im-portance.

Some CEOs cement their position using an explicit process of:

- Identifying the stakeholders who are in a position to influence their success (both inside and outside the company)

- Assessing the issues of most concern to each stakeholder, the importance of that stakeholder's co-operation and the relationships between stakeholders

- Setting out a stakeholder management plan to deal with each of the more important stakeholders.

Probably the most critical stakeholder groups during this period are within the company: directors, managers and staff. The last two groups, in particular, have an enormous incentive to understand the nature of the new CEO, and every move will be scrutinized. Even such innocuous activities as taking lunch will send a signal: do you eat with staff, managers or customers? Do you work through lunch or take a break? Is your lunch frugal or extravagant? Such trivia can shape your brand.

During the first six months, especially, you can send very powerful sig-nals to the organization without really doing anything. Sending the right signals depends on having a clear idea of the existing culture of the business, being clear about the signals you want to send and being dis-ciplined in your own behaviour to ensure that you send only the signals you intend to send.

If you send the wrong signals, and fail to attend to the important constituencies within the company, you could soon be out of a job. One, ultimately unsuccessful, CEO took charge of an electronics company in a blaze of publicity and with a rich options package. He spent his early months assuring stakeholders that, because of his track record, perform-ance was bound to improve. For the first few months he appeared to be right as the share price moved sharply upwards.

Perhaps sensing victory within his grasp, however, the CEO failed to take the time to convince managers that he actually understood the business he was now running. Instead, he repeatedly drew their attention to the share price and to the value he had 'created'. Disaffection among senior executives soon spread to the boardroom. One day short of a year after taking office, and the CEO was out.

A well-thought-out approach to understanding the issues, therefore, is an essential foundation for longer-term success.

Justin King, CEO of Sainsbury's: the first 100 days

Justin King is keen to point out that 100 days is a metaphor, not a reality – and that the metaphor can be dangerous if it sets an expectation that major change will have been completed in the first 100 days. 'In any case,' he says, 'I had three first 100 days! First of all was the period of my gardening leave in 2004; then I had what really was my first 100 days; and then in early July, I started another key period to complete the business review.' He spent each of these periods in quite different ways.

During the first period, he was unable to exercise any executive role, but he was allowed to go shopping in Sainsbury's stores and in those of its competitors. His focus was to understand as well as he could the situation of the business from three perspectives: customers, colleagues and competitors. Having been active in the sector for many years, he learned little new about competitors – but he learned a great deal about Sainsbury's. Visiting 50 stores, seeing the condition of each, and the pricing strategy confirmed his feeling about the business problems faced by Sainsbury's – but talking to colleagues gave him a sense of something he had not known: the depths of despondency to which his 150,000 future colleagues had sunk. He realized that since the departure of Lord John Sainsbury, the business had lacked real clarity of leadership, and determined that his own style would have to be high profile, to communicate clear messages right from the start.

Once he arrived, on 29 March 2004, he found two cultures: senior management in denial about the depths of the issues, while those on the shop floor were deeply concerned. He also found that the business was in operational crisis, brought on by a series of decisions which, by denying the depths of the problems and attempting to postpone the day of reckoning, had compounded the underlying issues. 'I decided I had to act fast.'

He began by announcing a major reduction in prices, followed shortly by a profits warning, telling the City: 'The level of profitability you have previously expected is not a realistic reflection of what this business is in a position to deliver.' One of the most encouraging signs in this period was the response King had to a 'personal' letter to 1 million Sainsbury's customers, of whom around 250,000 took the time to write back with their comments on the business. This confirmed the extraordinary well of customer loyalty from which – despite its recent poor performance – Sainsbury's was still able to draw. In July, King was able to say, effectively: 'This business has big problems, but it is fixable. Give us until 19 October, and we will tell you how we are going to fix it.'

The third 100 days was the period from 1 July to 19 October, which was spent developing the 'Making Sainsbury's Great Again' business plan, and in reshaping the senior management team – a good number of which have been replaced with people King knows and in whom he has absolute confidence: perhaps the strongest team in UK retailing. One consequence of this clear-out was that there was a period in August when 'I was doing three jobs, the new people had not arrived – that was a stretching time!' On 19 October 2004, he launched 'Making Sainsbury's Great Again' almost simultaneously to staff and shareholders. The plan was well received by both, and has been delivering impressively both in operational terms and in rebuilding sales and service levels.

Building your team

The point has been made elsewhere that a strong team is essential for success. The first 100 days is the ideal time to assess and restructure the team: 100 days is long enough to assess whether your colleagues have the skill and will to deliver the performance you require, but it is short enough to prevent strong loyalties building up which make it hard for you to act.

While speed is essential, making the right decisions is even more important – give yourself time to assess your team in the round; some managers do not make a good first impression but can be relied upon to deliver and vice versa. Similarly, if commitment is to be part of the decision, you need to allow them the time to commit – some highly skilled managers are reluctant to make an instant commitment; they first reflect and then commit. Finally, it takes time to assess your team as a team, rather than just as individuals. You need them to be willing and able to pull together.

Mervyn Davies, CEO of Standard Chartered Bank: the first 100 days

Mervyn Davies, CEO of Standard Chartered Bank, took control at a difficult time. He did not have the luxury of taking stock; in fact he had a number of fires to extinguish quite quickly. Within the first four weeks, he recognized that he needed a new CFO, and acted on this well within the first 100 days.

Nevertheless, the focus of his initial activity was listening: 'I travelled like a maniac; people thought I was crazy. I visited 20 countries in three months, places I didn't know. I ran clinics with staff, I spoke to those I trusted two or three levels down in the organization, I listened to the views of outsiders. I made sure I understood what was really wrong, and what was our challenge.'

After four weeks he called an emergency meeting of top management. 'We got the outsiders to tell us what they really thought: two analysts, two investors and one adviser. Out of two days of review came a recognition of our challenge, a commitment to a stretch target – this is really important – and a sense of urgency without panic.'

A big part of the challenge Davies identified was cultural: 'We had stopped having courageous conversations. I took three other significant actions in that 100 days:

- I launched a leadership course for senior managers to get them to understand and step up to their ability
    - to influence the business
    - to grow and develop themselves.
- We had a "Customer Week" where everyone who was not already customer-facing had to stop whatever they were doing – even me – and spend a week listening to customers. (For some people, that meant their internal customers.) It was a great success and led to an explosion of creativity.
- We ran a "Eurovision Song Contest". Every unit in the business had to enter at least one team, though some had multiple entries. They all sang the same song, "I Believe I Can Fly". This really helped everyone to feel part of the same one company, and it has led to a more creative atmosphere.'

That wasn't all. 'After that, we published our Management Agenda

– externally first – to set out our commitment to our shareholders,' said Davies. 'We have set out seven key points that we will deliver. This has created space for us to create the future. It's very important not to over-promise.

'At the end of the first year, using a coach I conducted a rigorous diary analysis to find out how much of my time was spent on the seven key agenda items. We have made some big changes to the structure of my time as a result.'

Building a team is not, of course, simply a question of selection. Aligning the team behind the goals of the organization may also be a significant task.

Setting the future direction for the business

In most cases, but not all, the first 100 days are principally a period for learning rather than action. Determining whether this applies to your business should be one of your highest priorities. If the business is haemorrhaging cash, customers or other critical resources, so that even its short-term survival is in doubt, there is no question: you must act first and learn later and a great degree of clumsiness is permissible in such circumstances. If, at the other extreme, you have inherited a sound business, even if you feel it could do much better, you must act with great care.

One of the main causes of early CEO failure is inattention to learning, which can result in failing to build a consensus around the desired direction and even choosing the wrong direction. Reviewing the contents of the earlier section on strong management may be helpful as a way of structuring the information gathering during this period.

Once you are confident that you have learned what you need to know about the business, the remainder of the 100 days should be spent in working out how to build a powerful coalition of stakeholders willing to commit to that new direction.

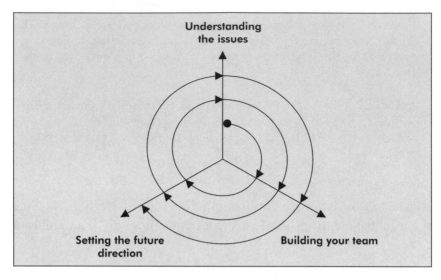

Fig. 28 Making progress on all three dimensions during the first 100 days.
Source: PA analysis

The three areas of activity outlined above are therefore not sequential, they march together in lock-step.

As Figure 28 suggests, careful management of your time is critical if you are to achieve the objective of creating a sound foundation.

Mike Frayne, former Executive Chairman of Intec Telecom: the first 100 days

When Mike Frayne bought the Interconnect product line from Sterling Software to create Intec Telecom, he had a product, 15 staff and eight customers – but not really a company. The product had been bought by Sterling a few months earlier from TI, and the disruption had destabilized staff, product and customers.

Frayne's first 100 days were therefore spent in crisis management.

The first priority was building trust with customers – to buy the time needed to stabilize the product. The second priority was stabilization: new people were brought on board, both on the technical side and with customer-facing skills. A focus on product quality and customer service started to drive Intec's actions.

During this stage, the business was very short of cash and a mentality of cash management and cost containment was developed, which has remained with the company even through the telecoms boom.

These two areas of focus paid dividends after a few nerve-racking months when Intec won its first new customer and a new lease of life. Intec Telecom rapidly became profitable, and had a successful IPO in June 2000.

Frayne offers the following advice to those about to start their first 100 days:

- 'Make sure you spend your time getting to know the heartbeat of the business
- If the business is in crisis, it will be one of three things: just fix that one (selling too little, selling the wrong thing or spending too much)
- Don't be carried away by the rate of change of technology
- Persevere.'

3 Dealing with underperforming businesses

Most business units will, from time to time, underperform. A corporation consisting of more than a dozen or so business units will probably have at least one or two underperforming at any time. As CEO, in deciding how to react to this underperformance, you have to strike the balance between dynamic action while bearing in mind that you have empowered a team to run that business, and made them accountable for results.

How and when should you intervene in such circumstances?

The CEO should act fast to assess the damage but intervene at the lowest level consistent with value delivery:

- You need to act fast to assess the damage because, unlike medical problems, 80 per cent of which heal themselves, most business performance issues will actually get worse over time.

- You need to intervene at the lowest level consistent with value delivery because the more active you are, the more you risk disempowering the management team – and this could have serious longer-term consequences.

Assessment

Assessing the damage

Management time, particularly your own time, is one of the most precious resources in the business. The first step in your assessment should therefore be one of materiality.

Consider whether the underperformance is material in the context of this business unit. Also question whether the underperformance is material in the context of the wider group. Does this business have the potential to create huge amounts of value for the group in the future that is being jeopardized by the current underperformance? Is the level of underperformance of this business weakening the financial strength of the group to a material degree?

If the business problem is not material – neither in the context of the business unit nor in that of the wider group – then you should ignore it. If you have good performance management processes in place, managers will be sufficiently encouraged to rectify the problem with no additional involvement of top management effort.

If the problem is material in the context of the business unit but not that of the wider group, you should expect to engage very lightly in its solution. Only if the problem is material both for the business unit and the group should you be prepared to invest significant amounts of your own effort.

Assessing the cause

If you decide that intervention is necessary, your first step should be to form your own view of the cause of the problem. To do this you must ask a series of questions:

- Is it simply a blip: a slightly larger than normal variation in monthly performance?

- Is it caused by an operational glitch, for example, a changeover to use of a new system that has delayed order entry?

- Is it simply the result of the business cycle and, if so, how long will the trough last and how deep will it be?

- Is the business model broken and, if so, is that because of fundamental shifts in the market or because of important moves by competitors?

- Is it simply the result of major mismanagement and, if so, does it stem from incompetence or something worse?

Assessing your managers' response

Finally, once you have assessed the issue, the next stage is to assess the managers' response to it. Do the managers understand why the problem has arisen? And if they do, do they know *where* the problem resides (in the sense of which geographies, which product groups, which customer segments, etc.)? Knowing the problem exists is one thing; being able to deal with it is another. Do the managers have a clear and logical plan based on the assessment, and are they acting on it? If so, does it look as if they are getting results within the timescale suggested by the plan?

Intervention

The nature of any intervention will be conditioned by the likely impact of the business problem and by your assessment of whether management will resolve the problem without intervention.

Where the business issues are material to the organization, you will need to intervene. First, you must drive understanding of the problem on the part of managers (note that this does not imply that you know the answer); then drive action based on that understanding; and, finally, if appropriate action is not forthcoming from the existing managers, change them (see Figure 29).

Where the problem is not material to the group, your intervention should, of course, be lighter; and you have the further option of simply exiting the business, if fully resolving the problem requires too much top management effort to be justified.

Challenge	Possible methods
Driving understanding	• Informal coaching • Demand set-piece presentation of analysis of issues. (Where is the problem? Why has it occurred? What is the scale of the impact? What are the options for response?) • Insist that a project be set up to investigate and report back
Driving action	• Informal coaching • Demand set-piece presentation of improvement initiatives • Set up task force with clear charter, access to top and strong membership
Strengthening management	• Second other managers onto task force • Replace existing managers

Fig. 29 Possible means of intervention.

Source: PA analysis.

4 Dealing with underperforming individuals

If this is a brief chapter, it is partly because the issue highlighted requires summary action – not, if at all possible, a lengthy, drawn-out protracted solution.

One of your top team is underperforming – not meeting targets, not making the right decisions and failing to lead the team effectively. What do you do?

If it is a junior manager then it is a straightforward issue. At least it is in the UK or the US where labour laws are still easier for employers than elsewhere. Step one is a good talking to; step two is a formal warning; and step three is a final written warning and, finally, dismissal. Within a year the problem has left.

Unfortunately, this process does not work for a member of the top team. Trust and confidence in the top team is vital. The minute that confidence is broken it is hard for the CEO not to second-guess decisions, question thinking, discuss shortcomings with other members of the top team and generally undermine the top-team individual concerned.

The correct process for dealing with an underperforming individual is to sit quietly, reflecting on:

- Did I make his or her objectives clear? If the answer is no, then make the objectives clear and try again.

- Is the underperformance really down to the individual's lack of ability? If the answer is no, then put your energy into making sure the external problem is solved.

- Can I replace the individual? If the answer is no, then make sure you can change it to yes as soon as possible.

If the answer to all three questions is yes, then dismiss the individual as speedily as you can, even if this means paying substantial compensation: these costs will be less than the costs of inaction. An alternative might seem to be to move the offending person to another part of the firm. But while this is a possibility, there are risks involved. They may, for example, behave in a negative way due to a sense of personal betrayal.

Instant dismissal may involve considerable costs. Nevertheless, it is better to pay up and then remember the pain during the next over-hurried recruitment interview and when planning the development of your remaining senior colleagues. Remember to follow three simple principles:

- You must have confidence in the ability of your top team

- There is no room for a remedial development plan for your top team

- Decide quickly and act quickly.

The high-performing CEO: Sir Terry Leahy and Tesco

Sir Terry Leahy started work at Tesco in 1979. Eighteen years later, he took over as the CEO of a company that, at the time, was lagging a long way behind its rivals and being deserted by its customers. Since then, not only has Tesco become the largest retailer in the country, and one of the largest in the world, but it passed the £2 billion profit mark in April 2005. Leahy puts his success down to a willingness to listen to the requirements of the customer and to train and develop his staff.

An early project discerned that customers did not appreciate Tesco emulating the approach of its major rivals such as Sainsbury's: instead, Leahy focused his efforts on developing a relationship with his customers that worked for Tesco. This was extremely successful – to such an extent that other retailers now attempt to copy it.

Unusually for a CEO, Leahy is from a marketing background. His approach to the management of the company placed an emphasis on marketing that led to the adoption of, and belief in, the current 'Every Little Helps'. There is a perception among the shopping public that Tesco begins with the need of the customer and works back from there to find the optimal business structure. In addition, if customer surveys suggest a requirement for a new line or product, the chances are it will be introduced.

Leahy was responsible for the introduction of both the 'Value' and 'Finest' lines of product, segmenting the products to appeal to all segments of the market. He also pioneered the Clubcard, initially written off by analysts and competitors, but then found to be a valuable source of consumer data and a powerful way of rewarding customer loyalty.

Tesco has recently made successful forays into the international market by partnering with local supermarket chains while providing its own supply chain and hardware systems. Its development of local staff to lead has assisted the success of the venture, as it has in the UK. Leahy's approach to staff development is typically hands-on: around one in ten employees are selected for further development. Across the company there is a clear and consistent framework for staff so that they are left in no doubt as to their role and how they can contribute.

In the future, Leahy has plans to continue to capture market share in both food and non-food arenas, including further expansion of the online retail store and a share issue to finance further international expansion. This is set against a context of exceptional TSR performance, with an annualized TSR of 18 per cent for the period 1994–2004.

5 Making mergers and acquisitions

Mergers and acquisitions have always been one of the most popular methods of growing a business.[1]

Over the last 20 years, there have been a large number of studies into the success rates of acquisitions, almost all of which have concluded that between 60 per cent and 80 per cent of acquisitions destroy value.[2]

While the worst cases stemmed from the diversification thinking of the 1970s – tobacco companies owning insurance businesses; oil companies buying mines; motor companies buying software houses – there are plenty of more recent examples where the logic merely seemed better.

Faced with this overwhelmingly negative picture, how should the CEO who wants to deliver shareholder value approach acquisition opportunities? Only by consciously aligning the emotional commitment of key stakeholders to the logic of value creation can you materially alter the odds of success.

The logic of value creation is actually very simple. It is often, however, obscured by the strength of the emotional commitment to doing the deal. To improve the odds of value creation, CEOs must consciously highlight the issue of value creation and weaken any misguided resolve for pursuing mergers and acquisitions at any cost by aligning the interests of the key stakeholders with value creation.

[1] Data from Thompson Financial, values M&A activity for 2004 at US$1.9 trillion.

[2] For example, a study by Marcum in 2003 found that 65 per cent of strategic mergers and acquisitions result in negative shareholder value.

The simple logic of value creation

The logic behind creation of value in an acquisition is simple, as illustrated in Figure 30.

Simply put, an acquisition creates value if the value received by the acquirer is greater than the value paid.

The value received is equal to the intrinsic value of the business on a stand-alone basis plus the value of the synergies, less the value consumed by the costs of integration. The value paid is the sum of the previous market value of the business plus the premium paid (often up to 40 per cent) plus the deal costs (often 2.5–5 per cent).

In the hypothetical example in Figure 30, the premium paid is 33 per cent of the previous market value and the synergies are 30 per cent of the intrinsic value (20 per cent when net of integration costs). In addition, the business was undervalued by the market (market value vs intrinsic value) by 20 per cent.

Even in this somewhat optimistic scenario, the value created is less than ten per cent of the price paid. It is not easy to create value.

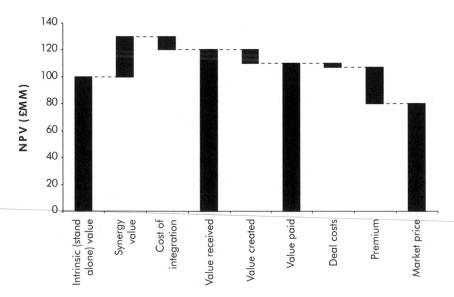

Fig. 30 Value creation in an acquisition.
Source: PA analysis.

Forces that obscure this logic

Despite the statistics, and despite the apparent simplicity of the value-creation logic, many deals are still done which destroy shareholder value. Why? In fact it is very difficult for CEOs to adhere to the logic of value creation for a number of reasons.

For a start, the CEO's own benefits package may be structured in such a way as to create an incentive to do a deal even at the expense of value creation. Equally, there may be pressure to go ahead from others, both within and outside the organization, whose rewards are driven by a deal occurring even at the expense of value creation.

There may be strategic imperatives, such as achieving a critical mass or becoming first or second in the sector, that make an acquisition seem attractive regardless of value creation. The metrics (turnover, profit and EPS) will often be flattered by even a poor acquisition, so the finances can often be presented in such a way that makes the acquisition seem attractive.

And then there is the psychology. Competitive pressures, doing the deal to stop competitors doing it, may lead to irrational decision-making, as can the simple buzz of making a conquest. An acquisition is an exciting, challenging activity to the extent that getting the deal done can often seem attractive with scant regard paid to the outcome.

Faced with this array of powerful pressures, it is a remarkably nerveless (possibly inhuman) CEO who can adhere clinically to the logic of value creation. Unfortunately, those who cannot, find they are doomed to join the value-destroying majority.

Aligning the interests of stakeholders

What can a CEO do to avoid this scenario? The solution lies in addressing the pressures that distort the value-creation logic, described above. Most of these pressures are either caused or reinforced by those with whom the CEO comes into contact during the pre-deal planning, including colleagues, non-executive directors, advisers and brokers.

Most of these stakeholders will, in addition to the CEO, have interests that are often misaligned with value creation, as shown in the table below.

Typical problem areas.

Stakeholder in deal	Interests
CEO	Salary based on size of business
	Deal-making rewards
	EPS-based rewards
Other colleagues	As for CEO
Non-executives	Small holding of company shares
	No value-based reward
Bankers	Paid a 'success fee' where 'success' simply means
	getting the deal done
Brokers	Paid on the basis of capital raised

Vodafone and Mannesmann

Vodafone chief executive Chris Gent received a bonus for his efforts in the acquisition of Mannesmann in 2000. The bonus was originally worth £10 million, half in cash and half in share options linked to performance. (The share options part of the deal was worth substantially less than £5 million by the time it was awarded in 2002.)

The bonus was tied to the £106 billion takeover rather than specifically to value creation. Many were critical of this move by the company's board of directors. At the EGM nearly 30 per cent of aggrieved shareholders registered their dissent by voting against or abstaining on remuneration resolutions.

Since the acquisition, the share price has fallen from a peak of '400 pence' to its current level of '120 pence', destroying huge amounts of value (see Figure 31).

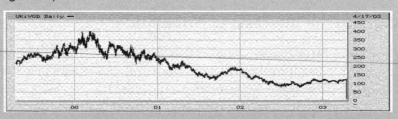

Fig. 31 The Mannesmann acquisition.

These issues can be dealt with by starting, before the deal process begins, to align and inform as many stakeholders as possible and to keep the remainder out of the centre of decision-making.

With respect to alignment, for example, as CEO you must check that your reward package provides you with an incentive to make value-creating acquisitions (and not any other kind). Close colleagues should be in similar types of benefit packages.

In jurisdictions where it is allowed, non-executive directors should have a significant holding of the company shares. If you need advisers in your inner circle, insist that their rewards do not come from simply making the deal happen, but from value being created over time.

On information, insist that at all times, the deal status and plans are presented according to the format in Figure 30, to make the value creation explicit to everyone. Of course, you must be aware of the pro forma impact on your accounts; you must know the impact on EPS – but do not mistake these things for the value creation of the deal.

There will always be stakeholders whom you cannot align and inform in this way: do not rely on them for advice on valuation or bid tactics.

Be prepared

Finally, to avoid value destruction, be prepared:

- **Pre-deal**, with a clear picture of how much value you expect to be able to add *in excess of that which other likely bidders can add*

- **Pre-negotiation**, with a clear negotiation strategy including an agreed walk-away price beyond which you will not go

- **Pre-completion**, with a detailed and fully resourced plan for taking control and integrating the business: many acquisitions fail to deliver planned synergies.

Appendix 1, strategy in the multi-business context, gives some useful guidance on acquisition strategy, while observation of successful acquirers shows that they have institutionalized the acquisition process into their business model. Few people are good at acquiring first time round.

6 Dealing with investors

The nature of shareholding has changed dramatically in recent years – and this causes a problem for managers. While most shares are still *held* by institutions like pension funds, most shares are now *traded* by hedge funds. Short-term prices are set by trading, and the result is that it is harder for managers to know those who set their short-term share prices.

Investors are becoming increasingly sophisticated and demanding. This increase in shareholder activism, coupled with an increased focus on corporate governance standards following the Enron, WorldCom and Xerox scandals, has had an impact on the role of the chief executive in terms of tenure and security of post.

This high turnover of CEOs is attributed, in part, to shareholders' desire for quicker returns, and a subsequent focus on quarterly results rather than on the longer-term direction of the organization. In addition, in the post-Enron world, investors are more sceptical than ever about the claims of senior management and their auditors.

To address these concerns, significant changes to corporate governance are under way. The Sarbanes-Oxley Act is generally seen as the most important piece of legislation affecting practices of financial disclosure, corporate governance and public accounting since the 1930s. The Act has introduced changes that affect not only US-listed companies, but also all companies wanting to trade in the US. One of the biggest changes to affect CEOs and finance directors is the increased personal responsibility as a result of the new requirement for them to sign off on the annual and quarterly reports.

Given the focus on short-term gains, the increase in shareholder activism and the corporate governance changes, CEOs must seek to build mutually beneficial relationships with shareholders and the investment community, while ensuring that their influence on the business is minimized. This can be achieved by focusing efforts on:

- Emphasizing the long-term strategic direction of the organization

- Defining the baseline intrinsic value of the organization

- Establishing the link to the organization's value drivers

- Effective and consistent value-based communications.

Emphasizing the long-term strategic direction of the organization

Some CEOs devote up to 20 per cent of their time preparing for and delivering briefings to investment analysts, journalists, fund managers and other investment professionals, yet many are dissatisfied with the outcome of these meetings as they feel that their actions are not accurately represented in analysts' reports or the financial media.

While some CEOs may feel that a series of meetings with the financial community is the only way in which to get their message across, others actively seek alternative routes thereby reducing the influence of the financial community on the organization. For example, Warren Buffett developed *The Berkshire Hathaway Owners' Manual* that details the organization's policies and values. This ensures that shareholders are provided with all the information they require to make an informed and rational judgement about the stock, which will in turn ensure that the stock price is logical.

Therefore, to reduce the pressure for short-term wins, CEOs should detail and communicate to investors the principles by which they will manage the company.

Defining the baseline intrinsic value of the organization

As we have said before, the overarching goal of the CEO is to maximize long-term shareholder value as measured (retrospectively) by TSR. For a shareholder deciding whether to buy a share, future TSR – which is what they really would like to know – is unavailable information. Instead, they can look at assessing the intrinsic value of the business, and compare this value with the current market value, as a guide. The CEO can help, or hinder, them in making this assessment.

Intrinsic value is an all-important concept that offers investors the only logical approach to evaluating the relative attractiveness of investments and businesses. *The Berkshire Hathaway Owners' Manual* defines intrinsic value as 'the discounted value of the cash that can be taken out of a business during its remaining life'.

The calculation of intrinsic value is not simple, and is sensitive to revisions of forecast cash flows, interest rates and sector risk. Furthermore, opinions differ on the most appropriate valuation methodology. Whatever methodology is adopted, the basic premise is that historical performance is analysed in order to forecast future performance over a particular horizon and a 'continuing value' beyond that horizon. Then, a cost of capital (equity) is estimated so that future performance can be translated into present value. Finally, the resulting valuation is tested for sanity and iterations are performed as appropriate.

In calculating its intrinsic value, the organization will have assessed the key internal and external factors that drive the value of the business. It is these factors, not the actual intrinsic value calculations, which should be communicated to shareholders so that they can make informed judgements about the organization. This is an approach that more and more companies are adopting as they try to shift the focus from achieving quarterly forecasts to long-term goals. For example, in December 2002, Coca-Cola decided that it would no longer provide any quarterly or annual earnings per share guidance; instead, it would provide investors with perspective on its value drivers, its strategic initiatives and those factors critical to understanding its business and operating environment.

Establishing the link to the organization's value drivers

Value drivers are so named because of their significant impact on the value of the business. Connecting them to a model of the business is not as complicated as it sounds, as there are generally a small number of hugely significant value drivers. For example, in the semi-conductor industry, utilization of foundry capacity will impact upon operational margin and cost values, whereas time to the release of the next chip will impact upon assumptions about future revenues and/or market profitability.

Having established where value is created in the business, it is important to make the link to the operational key performance indicators (KPIs), by which most managers make decisions and manage performance.

Having defined the value drivers and linked management's performance to the achievement of them, a CEO can communicate a clear message internally and externally about the future direction of the organization.

Effective and consistent value-based communication

Organizations that have been able to follow the previous steps should be well equipped to provide shareholders with an informed view about the long-term direction of the organization and provide them with the facts that they require to make an informed decision about the organization.

The information needs of the different audiences (for example, staff, institutional investors and private investors) should also be considered. The framework given in Figure 32 illustrates how the data can be represented in a way that addresses the interests of long- and short-term investors, management, employees and other stakeholders.

The framework reflects contemporary governance expectations by distinguishing between external and internal communication require-

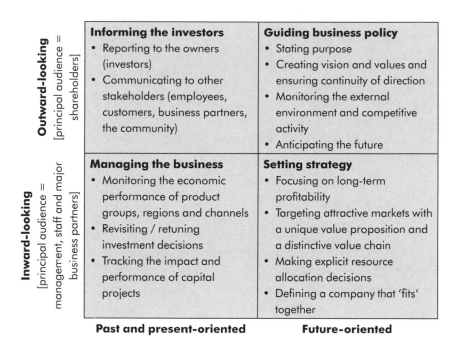

Fig. 32 Investor relations framework.
Source: PA Consulting Group.

ments, and between the need for information about the past and perspectives on the future.

By adopting this value-based approach to investor relations, the organization will benefit by ensuring that shareholders are provided with all the facts that they require to make informed decisions about the organization's long-term direction. In addition, by seeking to communicate directly with the shareholders, the influence of third parties can be minimized. Finally, it is important to note that new research by Harvard Business School has found that those organizations that were most responsive to shareholders in the 1990s enjoyed returns 8.5 per cent higher per annum than those run as management dictatorships.

7 Knowing when and how to go

If you read the book, put the processes in place, get the right team beneath you, design a world-class business model and double the value of the company in five years, then congratulations.

What is more, the investors will trust you and listen attentively to your plans and projections at each round of investor communication. They will all believe you and, as a result, they will have priced into the current share price their own predictions for continued growth and wealth creation.

This is a problem. Why? Because if this is true then the future total shareholder return will only be equal to the cost of equity (for a mathematical proof turn to Appendix 2). It means that it will take you at least seven years to double the value again. Faced with this, what do you do?

Renewing the challenge

Our belief is that there is always a better strategy. No business model is perfect so, by definition, there must be a better strategy. But this does not mean that you are necessarily the best person to steer the company in a new direction.

It is your job as CEO to evaluate the company and decide whether you are the person to lead the next round of change. In evaluating whether that option is available to you there are a number of specific questions you might ask.

Have you got the right management information? Do you really understand what regions, products and customer segments are delivering value? Do you really understand your competitors, how you perform in comparison, which is the cost leader in your market, how do they do it and can you do it better?

Do all key employees have their remuneration linked to the generation of shareholder value? Do all your employees understand the vision of the company and the importance of value-based management? Do your suppliers embrace the principles of value-based management?

Do your investors really understand your strategy? Do they have the information available to them to properly determine the intrinsic value of the company?

If the answer to any of these questions is no, you have the opportunity to stay and carry on the fight; even though the next doubling of value could be a good deal harder than the first. There is always a better strategy. We have yet to find a CEO who did not think things could be improved.

We asked Rolf Börjesson, then CEO of Rexam, a leading UK engineering firm, how the company could be different. 'My colleagues tell me I am never satisfied. We know how to satisfy shareholders for the next five years but I always want it faster, better. I worry about strategy every day. Mostly it is a debate I carry on with myself as drawing others into the debate can be unsettling if these thoughts are misinterpreted.'

If you are not the right person to take the company forward, then it is far better to step down. You have been a good CEO. CEOs are judged on their results. There is a shortage of good CEOs; therefore, you will be picked up quickly.

Most CEOs tend to agree that the optimum length of time in the post is around ten years. Michael Krasny, founder and CEO of CDW from 1984 to 2001 told me that after that time a CEO gets stale and ceases to know where the next major advance is going to come from. 'Being comfortable is not a good place to be. I was too satisfied – I had to go.'

A successful succession

After all those years building a successful company and great reputation, the thoughts of the complete CEO understandably turn to the issue of succession and legacy.

'Ten years is about right,' said Michael Critelli, CEO of Pitney Bowes, regarding the length of tenure. 'The first two years are spent solving the urgent problems and figuring out a strategy for the future, the next five to six years are spent implementing that strategy *and the final two to three years are spent grooming a successor.'*

Grooming a successor is more difficult for some than others. It is the hope of every CEO to leave the company in good hands, trusted hands, hands that have been guided by the CEO him or herself. But analysis shows that only 73 per cent of the CEOs of the FTSE 100 were appointed from within. Why is this the case?

Our feeling is that many successful CEOs suffer in this area from the very attributes that made them and their companies a success. How easy is it to groom a successor if you are always dissatisfied?

And weak CEOs could well be worse. Egocentric, insecure CEOs often feel threatened by those beneath them who begin to exhibit the capabilities and confidence of a CEO.

Grooming a successor requires maturity, understanding and strong coaching skills. Critelli commented that a successor has to look credible in the eyes of the board and the board is looking for someone with a vision, who is visibly competent and who can work with the people in the team. The CEO must assist in the process of building this credibility.

There are a number of key points that CEOs should consider when it comes to the issue of succession.

First, succession is vitally important. Choose the wrong successor and your legacy will be tarnished, and your shareholders will suffer. In one of the most publicized successions in corporate history, after years of planning, GE CEO Jack Welch handed over to Jeff Immelt who, although different in style, has continued the success of his predecessor.

Succession is not easy. In fact, it is rather difficult. Go outside the company and you have a higher risk of failure than if you choose an insider. Yet at times that risk may be worth taking. Bringing in Lou Gerstner to run IBM was an inspired, though very risky, decision: he didn't even know the industry well. If you choose an insider, you will also have to negotiate some major political hurdles within the organization, as there will be several contenders (at least in their own minds) and if they are not selected, they may well leave.

Being a brilliant number two is not necessarily an indicator of being a great number one. Just because they have managed well for shareholder value in the business you have built does not mean that they will continue to resist the temptation to choose another, easier path once you are gone.

Finally, good succession planning is systematic, and ongoing. You do not solve the problem by thinking 'I'm 18 months from retirement, I had better start thinking.' Instead, develop many strong candidates – for all key jobs – from among your talented younger managers, and stretch and develop them over a long period, so that they are truly qualified through their experience and knowledge as well as their talent.

And, as for you, whatever the challenge you take on next, good luck.

Part 4

The CEO's Toolkit

A quick glance at the CEO turnover statistics confirms that the job of the CEO is a tough one. There are, however, some tools that make the CEO's life a little easier. The fourth and final part of the book sets out a number of tools that are both proven to be effective and likely to be relevant to every CEO at some point.

The selected tools address:

- Section 1: Knowing yourself

- Section 2: Defining the information you require to enable yourself and your colleagues to manage the business effectively

- Section 3: Solving 'bet-the-ranch' problems

- Section 4: Driving significant change through the business

- Section 5: Time management.

1 Knowing yourself

In ancient Greece, visitors travelled from hundreds of miles to the Oracle at Delphi so that they could ask the Delphic Sibyl, the priestess of Apollo, to divine their future; usually in the hope of love, money or children. They were greeted by a sign urging them to 'Know thyself'.

The inscription was a reminder of a timeless truth. Our future depends very much on where we are now, and that in turn depends very much on who we are.

As discussed in the section on leadership, self-awareness is a must for every CEO. Who we are has a direct effect on what we do. In turn, what we do dictates the impact we have on others. If we truly know who we are, then we can understand and control our actions more effectively – and we can hope that those around us will respond more positively.

Who we are is a complex issue that few of us ever really understand. There are many factors that shape our identity: the environment we grew up in, the way in which we were brought up, our schools, our culture and, most importantly, our experiences.

So how do CEOs ensure that they know who they are – and stay updated with any changes?

There are three key things they should undertake to make sure that they stay in touch with who they are: psychometrics, listening and coaching.

Psychometrics

Just as there are many factors that make up who we are, there are many different personality types that make up the essence of who we are.

The classification of personality types has been going on a long while. Back in 400 BC Hippocrates classified the following types based on the predominant body fluid or humour: blood – sanguine (optimistic); black bile – melancholic (depressed); yellow bile – choleric (irritable); and phlegm – phlegmatic (listless and sluggish).

Things have progressed since then and more useful, and certainly more scientific, classifications now exist. One of the best is the Myers-Briggs Type Indicator (MBTI).

MBTI was developed by Isabel Briggs Myers and her mother, Katharine Cook Briggs. Their aim was to create a tool to indicate, validate and put to practical use the work on psychological types by Swiss psychiatrist Carl Jung.

Jung was a pupil, friend and colleague of the psychoanalyst Sigmund Freud (although the two eventually fell out). In 1921, Jung published his ideas on personality in his book *Psychological Types*.

Briggs Myers and her mother first encountered Jung's ideas in 1923 and began two decades of 'type watching'. Prompted by the waste of human potential in the Second World War, Myers began developing the Indicator to allow everyone to benefit from a better understanding of psychological type and to appreciate differences between people's personalities.

Briggs Myers concluded that each of us has a principal way of operation with respect to our flow of energy; how we take in information, how we make decisions and the everyday lifestyle we lead.

Within each of these categories we prefer to be:

• **Extroverted or Introverted**

- **S**ensing or i**N**tuitive

- **T**hinking or **F**eeling

- **J**udging or **P**erceiving.

Individuals are naturally more comfortable with one or other of these modes of operating:

- Our flow of energy – how we receive our stimulation – either internally or externally

- How we take in information: how do we absorb information – by trusting our senses to take it in or by trusting our intuition?

- How we make decisions: do we make decisions by utilizing objectivity and thought or do we trust our personal subjective value systems?

- The everyday lifestyle we lead: on a day-to-day basis do we prefer to be structured and organized (judging) or laid back, relaxed and open (perceiving)?

Taking the test will result in a score indicated by a four-letter MBTI personality type denoting the individual's preferences – ESFJ, for example, denotes an extroverted, sensing, feeling, judging individual. Numbers next to the letters indicate their weighting. The MBTI instrument is regularly updated to reflect the latest research in type theory. Data for over 4000 research studies provides a robust empirical foundation for the test and it is used by over 3 million people annually.

This is not the place to go into a detailed analysis of the different 'brain types'. It is worth saying that no type is right but on some occasions one type will be more effective than others. Clearly when evaluating an investment decision, thinking is more appropriate than feeling. When planning a large change programme, Js will do better than Ps, but when implementing it and motivating others, Ps might well be superior to Js.

The trick is to know yourself so well that you put effort into developing the more unnatural side of your personality and to know more easily when to delegate tasks to better suited people. Sure, you don't have to be an E to be an effective CEO but if you're an I then make sure you have an E in your team.

All that is true but there is nevertheless a higher incidence of ENTJs among CEOs than other types.

Listening

Earlier we explained how important it is that the CEO listens to the staff, the customers and the shareholders. However, that was in large part listening to views on the company, the products, the processes and the competition. As CEO you also have to listen hard to what people think about you. That includes your staff, your colleagues, and your friends and family as well as the world at large.

The people with the most cast-iron ego rarely take the role of CEO. In fact, some say that most CEOs are driven by a degree of personal insecurity. It is always hard to be objective about yourself. It is important to retain balance; perception is reality but you must find a way to detach your feelings from it.

Probably the most important person to listen to is your partner. He or she is one of the few people who can tell you when you have been foolish or mean or selfish. And he or she is usually right.

Coaching

A coach or mentor is a must, whether professional or not. Almost without exception the best CEOs find someone external to their organization that they can rely on who will listen attentively and give objective advice, all the while guaranteeing total confidentiality.

Executive coaching has become an industry in its own right. But a key requirement is that any coach needs to be someone that you look up to and admire. You have to have complete confidence that your coach has experienced the problems you are facing – and learnt from them. An experienced CEO or ex-CEO is probably best, but probably not a CEO who has worked for the company that you run. He or she will find it hard to be entirely objective.

The coach can help in two ways: helping you understand your own strengths and weaknesses but also practical advice on how to do the job.

Mervyn Davis, CEO of Standard Chartered Bank, tells of an experience with his coach. One of the biggest problems facing any CEO is time management. At the end of the year his coach suggested they do a detailed analysis of his diary for that year. It was clear that he was spending too much time with some groups of people and not enough with others. Often a one-hour meeting consisted of less than 30 minutes of content and more than 30 minutes of chinwagging. He completely re-engineered his use of time including, wherever possible, reducing the length of a meeting to 30 minutes.

'Nothing too much'

The inscription at the Oracle at Delphi said 'Know thyself' but followed this with another Delphic inscription: 'Nothing too much'. Wise advice indeed. CEOs cannot afford the luxury of endless self-analysis. Their job is to make good decisions and lead others in carrying them out. They need to know enough about themselves to capitalize on their strengths and compensate for their weaknesses. That and no more is necessary. Greater self-knowledge will bring no gain in performance. They will not be better CEOs for agonizing like Hamlet before every decision. As we have stressed before, ultimately CEOs are judged by the shareholders for *what* they do, not *who* they are.

2 Defining the information you require

Confidence in decision-making comes largely from confidence in the adequacy of the information on which those decisions are based. Most CEOs find themselves drowning in data – but have difficulty in getting the *information* they feel they need to drive the long-term performance of the business. This problem can best be resolved by identifying a simple set of information to support performance management and planning, and forcing the organization to provide it.

The CEO's dashboard

This dashboard consists of 12 charts, which between them will help you manage the business well. Most CEOs see only a part of this picture. Give yourself an advantage: call in your CFO, your head of IT and your marketing or strategy director and give them three months to produce the first version.

The dashboard has three components.

Value delivery – the acid test, but backward looking

For each SBU, CEOs should, on a monthly basis, be able to check a number of things.

First, they should be able to tell *how much* economic value is being created, and what the trend is. They should also be able to tell *where* that value is being created: in which product groups and business lines, and from

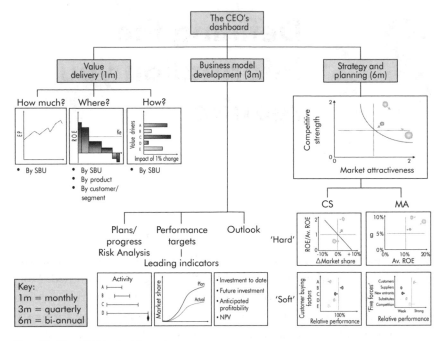

Fig. 33 The CEO's dashboard.
Source: PA analysis.

which customers or market segments. It is also important to know *how* the value is being created. What are the key value drivers for the SBU for example? What is performance against them?

Business model development – both retrospective and forward looking

Business model development shows how well the organization is preparing itself for the future.

In general, there will be some ongoing activity to refine the business model. On a quarterly basis at least, the CEO needs to track a number of factors to understand whether this activity is bearing fruit.

These fall into four main areas:

- What is the progress against plans? To assess this, the CEO should ask: What activities are planned? Who is responsible for these activities? And what progress has been made in these activities?

- What are the risks and issues involved? Answering this will mean considering risk assessment and the proposed mitigation of any risks.

- Is the business achieving its performance targets? The CEO must monitor the leading indicators of the performance of the future business model, including market share actual vs planned; cost/unit actual vs planned.

- Finally, the CEO must gauge the outlook. Questions here include What is the investment to date and what investment is still required? What is the profitability forecast? What is the implied NPV?

Strategy and planning – entirely future oriented

If the business is delivering value well, and the refinements to the business model have a positive outlook, it is tempting to feel that all is well – tempting, but very dangerous.

Our research has shown that successful businesses live on the edge of paranoia – many CEOs even inject it deliberately. Bill Gates, Chairman and Chief Software Architect at Microsoft, famously said: 'At any time, Microsoft is just two years away from bankruptcy.'

Living on the edge of paranoia requires the CEO to have a well-grounded view of what might go wrong strategically: Will the market cease to be attractive? Will low-cost competition destroy our profits?

There are a few simple facts to be understood:

Competition
Hard factors: Are we getting higher or lower returns than our competitors? Are we gaining or losing market share as we do so? What is our relative cost position?

Soft factors: What new moves are competitors making? How do we stack up against our toughest competitor in meeting our customers' key buying criteria? What are the trends?

Market assessment

Hard factors: How fast is the market growing? Will this rate decline? Is there a true (economic) profit to be earned in this market? Is the rate of profitability declining?

Soft factors: Michael Porter's 'Five Forces' (customer bargaining power, supplier bargaining power, threat of substitutes, threat of new entrants, and degree of competitive rivalry): How does the market look today? Which of these forces will intensify and by how much? PEST (political, environmental, sociological and technical): What threats are we facing?

All of these issues should be debated by the top team every six months – or at the very least, annually.

Reacting to warnings

When the dashboard blinks a warning what do you do? Ignore it and fix the problem at the next regular service? Drive cautiously to the next garage? Or get out of your vehicle right away? There are two logical possibilities and the answer flows from them.

Either your company's performance is still on track, or close enough, in all three key areas: value delivery, business model development and strategy and planning. In that case, operate through the CEO's high-performance model to make sure that you stay on track.

Or there is a serious problem. This requires rapid action. Does the problem stem from underperformance? Does it threaten the future of the company? Then go to the next section, on solving 'bet-the-ranch' problems.

3 Solving 'bet-the-ranch' problems

As CEO, you have to solve problems every day. They are all important, or you would not be dealing with them at all, but ultimately most of them are a question of applying existing policy, or delivering existing strategy. For example, resolving tensions between two business unit heads, or addressing an issue of underperformance in a small subsidiary. Being right 80 per cent of the time is more than acceptable in these areas.

Once a year, however, a more fundamental problem arises. A problem where a major commitment must be made and where the costs of getting the decision wrong are material to the business. In such a case the stakes are dramatically higher: you have to act, but you cannot afford to be wrong. A 20 per cent chance of error is too high.

So how should you approach such problems? Successful CEOs treat these problems very differently:

- First, they take care to **define the issue clearly**

- Then they **develop a complete set of concrete options for response**

- Finally, they **find enough facts to give them confidence to act**.

Define the issue clearly

A crucial first step is to clarify the issue. To get to the right solution in a reasonable time frame, you must determine the action question that must be answered, be clear on the basis on which the decision will be made and focus clearly on the big-bet elements of the issue.

Action question

It is important to set out an action question which, if answered clearly, will give an explicit basis for concrete action. Let us take, as an example, an issue that many CEOs mishandled: the auction for third-generation (3G) mobile telephone licences. The first step is to define the action question. Is it: How much should we bid? Should we bid? Or: How should we approach licence acquisition?

The first question assumes that a bid is the right strategy and an answer to the question, therefore, gives no guidance on action in the event of competitors bidding higher. Although the second question has the advantage of opening the mind to strategies other than bidding, an answer to the question might not give much concrete guidance.

The third question is more powerful than either of the other two: it opens the mind to a range of strategies and is phrased in such a way that an answer will be a useful guide to action.

Basis of decision

Next, it is important to be clear about the basis on which the question should be answered. In the auctions as they took place in the UK, it seemed as though bidders had decided that they *had* to have a licence at any cost short of bankruptcy. The implicit basis of decision-making might have been the likelihood of different strategies resulting in a licence being acquired.

A high-performing CEO would, of course, have taken a decision based on the impact on long-term shareholder value. Even this, however, requires further clarification. Suppose that loss of a licence to a competitor might result not only in the loss of a future profit stream from 3G but also in material damage to existing businesses. The net impact on long-term shareholder value is then the combination of value created/destroyed through acquisition of the licence and the value protected in the other affected businesses.

Focus very clearly on the big-bet elements of the issue

Many strategic questions have an element which is big-bet, but other elements which need not be. There can be very high value in distinguishing them. In the retail world, for example, introducing a new store concept across all stores is a major strategic move – getting it wrong could be disastrous – but it need not be a 'bet-the-ranch' issue. Retail managers would elect to pilot a new concept in a small but significant sample of stores, testing it in the market directly instead of via research or analysis. The failure of such a pilot would be a regret but not a disaster.

Develop concrete options for response

Once the issue is clear, you need to develop a range of possible solutions.

Open approach to solutions

Given the stakes, you must be careful not to overlook the best solution simply because it represents a change in focus or mindset: you must be open to the best solution.

Returning to the 3G licence auctions, the behaviour of the participants strongly suggests that they were considering only two possible courses of action. Either they were going to bid high enough to win the licence – and then seek to operate it profitably – or, alternatively, they would bid lower and accept that the 3G boat had sailed.

Seeing the world this way means that other strategies may be missed completely and that the second outcome seems so undesirable that the first one looks good under almost any circumstances.

A number of other options might have been worth considering beyond the two more obvious choices. A company anxious to acquire a 3G licence might have done so by buying a competitor that had already successfully bid for one in an auction. It might have sought to establish a co-sharing alliance with a successful bidder. Alternatively, thinking a bit more laterally, the company could aim to compete against 3G by using 2.5G technology as long as possible and then leapfrogging to 4G.

Finally, it might seek to alter the nature or structure of the auctions. Involving non-experts in generating ideas can be very valuable: they are less likely to fall victim to group-think.

Identify all your degrees of freedom

One way of opening the mind is to try to identify all the levers available to managers: the degrees of freedom in finding a solution.

In the case of the 3G auction, the degrees of freedom included level of bid, approach to lobbying, acquisition strategy, alliance strategy and technology strategy. All of these degrees of freedom should have been evaluated thoroughly.

Create hypotheses for action

Next, for each of these degrees of freedom management the CEO should then identify a hypothesis for action. Between them, these hypotheses, if proven true, would then constitute a strategy for action.

In the 3G example there are a number of possible hypotheses.

The CEO might decide that the walk-away level of the bid should be set to equal the net present value of the proposed 3G business less the network investment required.

The bid may go higher than the company is prepared to pay, and as a result the company's bid will be unsuccessful. In this case the assumption may be that the successful bidders have overpaid and acquiring a successful bidder via the stock market will provide a better bargain than the auction.

Other hypotheses might include seeking to make alliances with other players, in effect to 'share' a licence, or finding alternative technologies that can compete with 3G.

The challenge then is to test these hypotheses to ensure that they represent a sound strategy. This challenge is complicated by the fact that all the important information on which these decisions should be based is information about the future while all the available information relates to the past – and the latter may not be a good guide to the former.

Find enough facts to give the confidence to act

You may need to work hard to uncover the facts on which you can base a sound decision, free from prejudice.

Avoid the danger of analysis for its own sake

Analysis of a complex question such as the strategy for 3G-licence acquisition is of course essential to sound management. It carries with it the danger of what is sometimes known as 'analysis paralysis': getting stuck into a never-ending loop of analysis. In the case of the licences, there was a clear deadline imposed by the auction process that prevented this. In other cases, management must guard against this danger.

Three guidelines can help:

Do not attempt to know the unknowable

There is a great temptation to try to know the unknowable. In the case of the 3G licences, armed with a crystal ball, the analysis would be easy: identify the top ten services by revenue in 2008, say; identify the running and capital costs associated with these services; calculate the profitability of these services. In the absence of the crystal ball, however, these data are unknowable and attempting to estimate them might lead to enormous errors.

Aim for direction, not precision

The licence auctions are a rare case in which precision could be valuable – it would tell bidders precisely the maximum bid they should offer. Even here, though, a mindset that says 'I want direction, not precision' would have two benefits: it reminds managers that there is more than one possible direction; it avoids the risk of attempting to create spurious precision – which more often leads to large error. As the economist John Maynard Keynes said, 'it is better to be roughly right than precisely wrong'.

One way to focus on the directional rather than the precise is to think constantly about 'what would need to be true for this to be the right response?' As we showed on page 125, for the bids at their actual levels to be justified, managers would have had to believe that either average revenue per user would be eight times greater with 3G than 2G; or the profitability of 3G would be eight times higher; or, of course, some combination of the two.

Analyse only what is strictly necessary – this will be quite large enough a workload

There is a powerful technique available to managers to help them to structure their problem-solving efforts to address the danger of over-analysis: it is called issue analysis.

The principles of issue analysis are simple:

- Phrase the issue you face as an action question (as described above)

- Create a full list of options for resolution (sometimes referred to as a MECE list – mutually exclusive and completely exhaustive)

- Phrase each of these options also as an action question

- Decompose these questions further into insight questions (questions whose answers give a valuable insight, but may not point to a concrete action themselves)

- For each insight question, identify facts that would enable you to create that insight.

The issue analysis is usually constructed as a hierarchical structure, as shown in Figure 34.

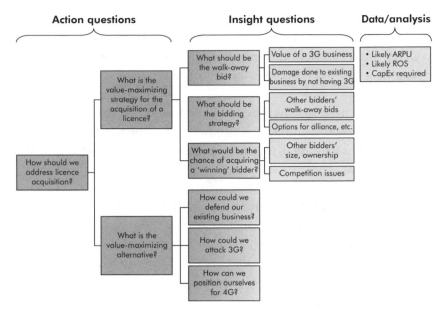

Fig. 34 Example issue analysis (partial).
Source: PA analysis.

There are several advantages to mapping out an issue analysis at an early stage in 'bet-the-ranch' decision-making.

In particular it allows the CEO to test the logic of the decision before it is made through asking a number of questions, even before all the data are available. If all the data were listed, would that answer all the insight questions? If there were answers to all the insight questions, would that in turn answer the action questions? Would answers to all the action questions then provide full guidance on how to respond?

Craft the answer into a clear call to action

Once you have the results and have determined the course of action to take, the challenge is in responding effectively. Here issue analysis can help again through making the logic clear and simple, and in painting a picture of the benefits of action.

Clear and simple logic

The issue analysis has a built-in logic, which means that you have armed yourself with precisely the information needed to confirm that the course of action you propose is the right one.

It may not be necessary to present *all* the results of your analysis – for example, a hypothesis that was unproven may be irrelevant to most audiences – but the core of the argument should be easily lifted from the results of the analysis.

Paint picture of status quo and benefits of future state

In getting an organization to change – and most 'bet-the-ranch' decisions will involve major change – you have to be able to motivate your managers and staff to make the change. Research by Professor Myron Trybus at MIT suggests that change will take place only if:

> Dissatisfaction with the status quo + attractiveness of the target state + clarity of steps to be taken > perceived cost of change.

So, motivating them to change requires the CEO to spell out each of these elements, so that people can see for themselves that the change is worth making.

This provides an important first step for driving the necessary change through the organization: an argument that can 'make it essential' to change.

4 Driving significant change through the business

When a CEO takes charge of a company there is usually an existing business model, existing management processes, an established culture and, quite possibly, dyed-in-the wool people doing what they have done for ages. In most cases significant change is required in order to build the company the new CEO wants. Change management and the ability to effect change is, therefore, an essential part of the CEO's toolkit.

The fifteenth-century Florentine politician and philosopher, Niccolò Machiavelli, once said: 'There is nothing more difficult to take in hand, more perilous to conduct, or more uncertain in its success than to take the lead in the introduction of a new order of things.'

Machiavelli was right – it is very difficult. So why were many of the successful CEOs we talked to so keen to do just that?

Sir Brian Pitman explained his view that a CEO must change the organization at least every three years. This may appear an odd approach. Surely change is a function of need, not time, but many CEOs seem to agree with Pitman's view.

Michael Krasny, ex-CEO of CDW, remarked, 'Show me a great company and I'll show you one that changes all the time.' It seems that not changing results in stagnation, stagnation leads to a loss of competitive advantage and that ultimately leads to poor results. Krasny believes that change energizes an organization and that after a while an organization becomes accustomed to change, and consequently is able to respond more rapidly to any new situation.

Orchestrating change could well be the most important thing a CEO does. Success and the CEO is a hero; failure and he or she will be out in weeks or months.

Given that you have decided on change, how do you go about it?

Change management

Figure 35 summarizes the methodology of change. In essence, the methodology breaks down into four distinct phases:

- Making it essential

- Making it ready

- Making it happen

- Making it stick.

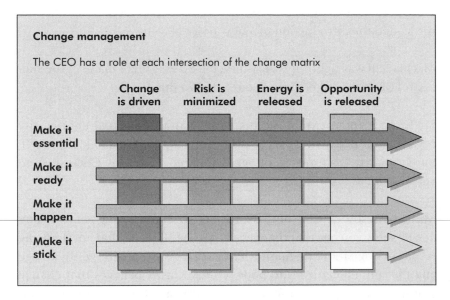

Fig. 35 PA's methodology of change.
Source: PA analysis.

Making it essential

At this stage the CEO is very much concerned with answering the question 'why do we need to change?' and 'what will be the high-level objectives of the change?' First of all the CEO must set up a team separate from the existing organization to perform the analysis. Why? Rolf Börjesson, CEO of Rexam, explained to us that the CEO cannot debate strategic options widely with the existing operational team; it causes disquiet and diverts attention from the everyday task of making money. Natural defence mechanisms also prevent the top team from really thinking 'out of the box' and exploring every possible avenue, however strange.

The CEO needs to develop a vision of change ready to communicate to the company. The vision should describe what is wrong at the moment, why change is really necessary, what is expected to happen once the change has taken place and the long-term vision of the future.

Attention must then be given to ensuring that everyone, and in particular the top team, understand the need for change.

Making it ready

Assuming the strategy is in place (if not, see Section 4) then crucial to this phase is the change design. This comes in four forms: physical design, organizational design, change programme design and communications design. The CEO is deeply involved in each area.

The physical design incorporates the customer proposition, the processes required to deliver it, the technology required to deliver it and also a model of the anticipated benefits and a timetable for their delivery. The CEO needs to be involved in the detail, understanding the model at every level, aware of the impact of every change, pushing the team to be more radical and understanding where value is created at every point. Great CEOs are not figureheads – they are detail junkies.

The CEO also needs to be heavily involved in the organizational design, particularly in the selection of those who will lead change activity. Care has to be taken in selection, as Figure 36 shows.

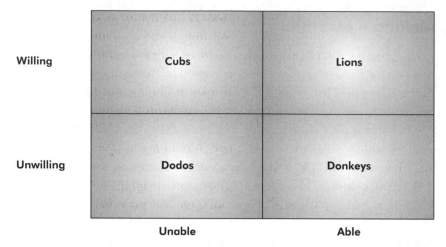

Fig. 36 Leaders of change matrix.
Source: PA analysis.

The most willing and able, the Lions, should be most involved in the change programme. The unwilling but able, the Donkeys, are best left at the coalface where they can busy themselves making money without derailing the change programme. Those willing but not yet able, the Cubs, should be reared as successor Lions. Dodos within the company, without will or ability, should be rendered extinct.

Designing the change programme can be left to specialists in that field but the CEO needs to have very close involvement. The CEO will ultimately carry the can for any failed change programme and his or her ownership is required.

Making it happen

Constant involvement is required throughout the execution of the change programme. The CEO must maintain morale among the troops, keep everyone onside and ensure that the benefits of the programme are brought out as early as possible. Regular communication with the company as a whole is the order of the day. Part of that communication is preaching tolerance. New processes, IT systems in particular, often have problems in the early days and there is always a temptation to use the lack of elegance or function in the new as an excuse to go back to the old.

Depending on the nature of the change, the CEO must ensure that appropriate project and programme management structures and processes are put in place.

The CEO must also check that the change progresses in accordance with his or her vision, keeping the programme on track at all times. The CEO can accelerate change by walking the walk and must be the first to adopt new policies.

Making it stick

Once the change is implemented there is always a danger that staff will slide back into the old way of doing things. The CEO is key to making sure that does not happen.

First, make sure that people are aware that the programme is complete. There are many ways of communicating this; an event to celebrate the achievement of the staff may be appropriate, for example. Most importantly, they need to know that they are entering a new phase of the company's history and that the pain is over.

A post-implementation review is also useful. It allows the CEO to ask: Who were the stars, who were the blockers and, more personally, as the CEO leading the change process, what did you learn and could you have done it better?

Make sure that as benefits are realized they are communicated widely. Each increase in sales or improvement in customer service will motivate the team to stick to the change and, hopefully, make them keener to embrace change again.

And the company must change again – regularly. As Michael Krasny wisely notes: 'What's right yesterday may not be right today. What's right today may not be right tomorrow and what's right tomorrow may not be right today. Don't be afraid of change.'

5 Time management

As CEO, you have the power to dictate the corporate agenda, to delegate at will and to recast all of the management processes. You can hire and fire and move people, you can launch new businesses and restructure or shut down established ones. But do you have control of your diary?

Unfortunately, most CEOs find that they do not. CEOs have to interact regularly with many different stakeholders. With some significant non-discretionary sinks of time, as well as a much more complicated set of priorities to juggle than other executives, how can CEOs manage their time in order to lead and manage their business effectively?

We believe that as a CEO you can make the best use of your precious time, and improve effectiveness, by using the high-performance model to focus on the real value-adding areas in your business.

To do this, you must:

- Use the model to define the areas and activities in which you do (and do not) want to spend your time

- Analyze your diary over a period of several months to find out how your time is actually being spent

- Determine how much time in your diary was spent by your choice and how much was imposed on you by having to follow a process (e.g. a board meeting) or responding to events (e.g. approving or making a public statement in an emergency)

• Take action to rebalance your time into the most valuable areas.

Using the model to define those areas in which you want to spend your time

There are three questions about time on which any CEO needs the assurance of a positive answer:

• Am I doing the right kind of thing?

• Am I interacting with the most important stakeholders?

• Am I spending my time on the most important topics?

To make your time management effective, you must analyze your diary in a way that enables you to answer these questions.

First of all, think about the major types of activity you could be involved with, for example, interacting with others with the objective of both managing and leading; working to your own agenda, time spent gathering ideas and information, reflecting, and reaching a decision; and less productive time such as that spent travelling and doing administrative tasks.

Moreover, even within a 'working day' you may well want to carve out some personal time – to phone family, buy a birthday present, or do any of the other things that make you a human being as well as a CEO.

Second, think about which stakeholders you believe are important to interact with, both internally and externally. One way to assess the importance of spending time with the different stakeholders is to consider the impact that their actions may have on the performance of the business as well as your personal ability to influence them. If both of these are high, it can be very productive to spend time with that particular stakeholder; conversely, of course, if both are low, your time could be better spent elsewhere.

Finally, but perhaps most importantly, you should think about which topics you wish to spend time on. Most CEOs have a value-creation agenda, which contains perhaps six to ten issues which they believe are the most critical for the organization at any one moment. In addition to this, you need to be sure that you spend the right balance of time looking forward to plan the way the organization will develop, and looking backwards on performance management to make sure that it is indeed delivering what it has promised.

Once you are clear about how you think you should be spending your time, you need to use these categories to begin analyzing how your time is actually spent.

Analyzing your diary

The figures below are based on an analysis of the time spent by a CEO during approximately 120 working days during his first year of tenure.

The high-level picture, shown in the table below, of total time by activity reveals a number of interesting features: the average working day was around 12.5 hours; only ten per cent of the time spent by this CEO was working on his own agenda, as distinct from interacting with others or being engaged in less productive activities; and almost one-quarter of the time is spent on less productive activities.

Total time by activity	%	Hours
Working on own	10	150
Interacting	67	1,005
Less productive	23	345
Total	100	1,500

Obviously this is an oversimplification: the 67 per cent of time spent in meetings with others, for example, is working time and the CEO may well have set the agenda. But it is not time that allows easily for reflection and for challenging the status quo. Less productive time is defined here as travel and pure administration: of course, not all of this can really be reduced, and indeed the CEO may well have made good use in many respects of the travel time – perhaps even for working. Nevertheless, an overall balance of 23 per cent less productive time and only ten per cent working time gives grounds to think about rebalancing.

If we turn to the analysis of time by topic, shown in the table below, we gain further insights.

Total time by topic	%	Hours
Non-key agenda items	18	270
Key agenda items but not CEO agenda	16	240
Travel	12	180
Administration	11	165
Unscheduled	10	150
CEO agenda: talent	7	105
CEO agenda: customer focus	5	75
CEO agenda: issue of the moment	5	75
CEO agenda: M&A	5	75
CEO agenda: investor relations	4	60
CEO agenda: government/regulators	4	60
CEO agenda: performance management	3	45
Total		1,500
Scheduled		1,350

For this CEO, all scheduled time was for meetings, administration and travel – and this accounted for almost 90 per cent, leaving very little time for reflection. Clearly, one option for him was to begin scheduling working time.

The biggest single area in which the CEO was spending time was on non-key agenda items, accounting for 18 per cent of the total. CEO agenda items, between them, accounted for only 33 per cent of the time with other key agenda items taking up a further 16 per cent. Within the CEO agenda items, performance management appears to be given very short shrift; of course, it is again possible that a lot of performance management activities were carried out under other headings, but far from clear that this CEO was able to give as much weight as he wanted to this key item on his chosen agenda.

Finally, looking at the stakeholders with whom the CEO interacted, we see from the table below that over half the time was spent with internal stakeholders, and of this, 44 per cent was spent with non-direct reports as against only nine per cent with direct reports.

Meeting time by stakeholder	%	Hours	Stakeholder	%	Hours
Internal	52		External	48	
Non-direct reports	44	229	Advisers	25	121
Executive directors	15	78	Others	18	87
Board	15	78	Customers	16	78
Committees	13	68	Governments	11	53
Direct reports	9	47	Investors	11	53
Other employees	4	21	Media	8	39
			Regulators	7	34
			Suppliers/partners	4	19
Total	100	521	Total	100	484

At first glance this looks like time misused: five times longer spent with non-direct reports than with direct reports, who were, of course, more senior people with more impact on the business. The key question is what the time with non-direct reports achieved. A charismatic leader, like this CEO, might have used his time to good effect in energizing large segments of the workforce to produce extraordinary results. But if most of that time was spent dealing with management issues in small groups, it was almost certainly inappropriate. In either case, nine per cent spent with direct reports seems very light, since interaction with senior people has such an important role in both management and leadership.

Of the 48 per cent of the time spent with external stakeholders, a quarter was spent with advisers. This gave them a greater share of the CEO's time than direct reports, which seems inappropriate. As much as 18 per cent of the time, more than any other external group except for advisers, was spent with 'other' stakeholders – not customers, not governments, not investors, not media, not regulators, not even suppliers. It seems very likely that some of this time is in fact less productive than it could be.

This CEO spent only about five per cent of his total time dealing with investors, which is very rare. Most of the CEOs we have worked with spend more like 15–20 per cent, and we found some CEOs who were spending as much as a quarter of their time dealing with investors. Those that spent less than ten per cent were usually fortunate in having a very small number of dominant shareholders, which made it much easier to communicate with them. However they managed it, those who spent less than ten per cent of their time dealing with investors freed a lot more time to spend actually running their businesses.

Time chosen or time imposed?

Analyzing your diary as described above should take you a long way to answering a revealing question: how much time do you spend as a CEO by your own choice and how much of it is effectively imposed on you? There are two principal ways in which your activities may be imposed on you: by process and by circumstance.

- *By process.* Any organization will have processes that take up your time as CEO. Some of these will be formal, such as board meetings or senior management meetings or staff-related processes, such as senior appointments, reporting and appeals. Some processes will be informal or customary but nonetheless carry obligations – such as attending staff parties or representing your organization at public events. Moreover, in any organization there will be a number of people with a 'customary right' to drop in on the CEO. Time spent with such people *on their initiative* is another source of imposition through process. It might of course be highly valuable – but it is not the way you chose to spend it.

- *By circumstance.* Other impositions on your time come from circumstance. The obvious examples relate to fire-fighting missions, damage control and dealing with emergencies. But there is another category that is less obvious and likely to be insidious. It arises when you have to spend time performing a task or dealing with a problem which someone below you should have done. It might be as trivial as replacing a light bulb; it might be as serious as tackling an internal problem in one of your organization's divisions or functions. Whatever it is, the task or problem has drifted up to you because those below lacked the competence, energy or authority to deal with it.

It is well worth analyzing both these kinds of imposition on your time. Each carries an 'opportunity cost' – the alternative use(s) you might have made of the time. Did they repay that 'opportunity cost'? Did they bring any value to you and your organization? Such an analysis may show you internal processes and customs in your organization that could be removed. As to impositions from circumstance, an analysis may well show you that there is not enough delegation in your organization or that there are people, or entire sections and units, not up to their jobs.

Taking action to rebalance your time

Having conducted this analysis, what can you do? There are at least three obvious areas which, between them, can make a large difference:

- *Diary management* enables you to set clear rules for how you wish your time to be allocated, and the duration and frequency of meetings with different stakeholder groups. This can cut out a lot of wasted time.

- Carefully reviewing *delegation* to make sure that as CEO you are spending enough time on the really critical issues is important. You should also think through carefully how you delegate not just management but also leadership and indeed less productive time.

- *Management processes.* In a well-functioning organization, the management processes should be set up to ensure that managers devote the right amounts of time, at the right time, to the key issues. If you find that you are not, or suspect that other managers are not, it is worth reviewing the management processes: both those looking forward – strategic and planning processes – and those looking backwards – performance management and reward processes.

There is also one vital appointment to make: your gatekeeper. Find someone you trust to manage your diary and appointments. This person will be firm enough to keep you on your chosen timetable and weed out timewasters, but tactful enough to avoid offending them. The gatekeeper will weed out unproductive time, ensure that everyone and everything is in place to make your meetings run smoothly and on schedule, and, perhaps most precious of all, protect you when you want to be alone and uninterrupted.

Time well spent

Ultimately, your effectiveness as a CEO will be determined by whether you spend your time doing the right things with the right people in the right ways; effective time management will be critical to your success.

Endnote

Now that you have read the book, we hope that you have a clear idea of the role of the CEO and the key actions which you can take to drive superior performance. We are well aware that although many of these things can be made to sound simple, in reality to do them well is extremely difficult. Nevertheless, we hope that, armed with the high-performance model as a guide, and with the support of the specific guidance on the CEO's challenges as well as the CEO's toolkit, you will be well placed to go forward and meet the challenge of leading your organization, division, business unit, or even team to a successful, high-performance future.

Appendix 1: Strategy in the multi-business context

Most of this book talks implicitly about single-business companies – we refer to having *a* winning business model, etc. – and for CEOs of most businesses, this is sufficient.

Some CEOs, however, run multi-business companies, where the business model resides at the SBU level, not at the group level – indeed the group itself may not have customers or competitors. How, in such a situation, should the CEO approach *corporate* strategy?

Everything in the book remains relevant for these CEOs, but it must be supplemented by one further fundamental concept. A sound corporate strategy must combine the ideas of SBU value creation, described earlier in the book, with the concept of parenting advantage:

- The SBU value-creation concepts tell you what should happen to each SBU to maximize value

- The parenting concept tells you who should do it

- In combination these concepts form the foundation of the corporate strategy.

The SBU value-creation concepts tell you what should happen to each SBU to maximize value

You will remember that a business can be in one of three states of value creation:

- Value destroying – when even conventional accounting is enough to tell you that the business is loss-making

- Value diluting – when the business makes an operating profit but an economic loss

- Value creating – when the business is creating shareholder value.

Of course, as we have pointed out before, a business that creates value today may not do so tomorrow, so a key task of strategy is to assess which of the businesses look as if they can be sustainably value creating. Once you have a clear future view of value creation, this is enough to give the following strong hypotheses, shown in Figure 37, about how best to maximize value creation.

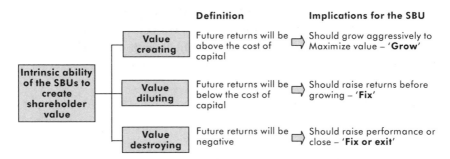

Fig. 37 Maximizing value in the SBU.

Of course, like all hypotheses, these will need testing.

The parenting concept tells you who should do it

The concepts of parenting advantage were developed by Goold, Campbell and Alexander, and set out in their book *Corporate Level Strategy*. The presentation of the issues here is our own, and differs in detail, though not in principle, from theirs. The core idea is simple, though the application is more subtle. Corporate strategy has to be able to answer questions about which business to buy and which to sell, and at what price. This means that the challenge of value creation in acquisitions becomes a central issue for corporate strategy. As we set out in the section on mergers and acquisitions, the logic of value creation through acquisition is simple but rarely followed. An acquisition creates value if the price paid is less than the value received. The price paid will usually reflect the results of a competitive auction of some kind – i.e. it will reflect the value other bidders are prepared to pay. The value received is simply the sum of the intrinsic stand-alone value of the business, plus the value of synergies the new parent can create, less the cost of integration and implementation of changes. This means that the ability of the corporation to buy in a competitive situation (which most are) and still create value comes down to its being able to create more synergy value than any alternative parent – this is parenting advantage.

Put at its simplest, if you do not have parenting advantage, and you nevertheless outbid rival parents in an auction, you will join the 80 per cent or so of companies whose acquisitions have destroyed value. What are the sources of parenting advantage? Only two:

- Horizontal synergies between different members of the corporate portfolio – e.g. merging operations or using the sales force of one business to distribute the products of another.

- Vertical synergies, where the parent can add value directly – e.g. by applying proven management principles to improve performance, for example, by implementing lean manufacturing, or by deploying the strong management disciplines we discussed in Part 2.

These vertical synergies have as their root the parenting characteristics of the business – and this is where the work comes in, to assess what value the parent can really add to its subsidiaries. These parenting characteristics are:

- Understanding of the market.

- Mental models of the business and knowledge of what interventions will create value. For example, a rule of thumb that says 'in a branded goods company, if share of voice falls below share of market, in general market share will start to fall off dramatically within 18 months' is a mental model that is extremely useful in those industries where it is true – but very dangerous if applied outside those industries.

- Specialist skills, for example, in lean manufacturing, technology, regulation, etc.

- Deal-making skills, which mean that the parent can add value by re-shaping the portfolio to the benefit of the members of that portfolio.

- Ability to intervene directly to improve business performance – e.g. by deploying the specialist skills of the centre to take out cost, or by providing central services to the business units.

- Ability to drive synergies between business units – e.g. in talent management.

Benchmarking these capabilities against those of rival parents will enable a business to create and validate a statement of the form:

> *In businesses with these defined characteristics (industry, type of operations, geography, type of customer, technology, etc.) we can create value using our parenting characteristics (as above) by taking these actions (e.g. sending in a hit squad to the factories, aligning rewards to creation of shareholder value, better operating back-office processes, better brand building, better serving the customers, etc.).*

From this understanding, the business can start to understand its parenting advantage: for which of the businesses it owns, or is thinking of owning, is it a good parent, and for which is it the best parent? (See Figure 38.)

This understanding gives clear hypotheses about ownership – one of the key questions of corporate strategy.

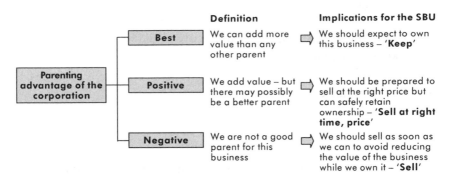

Fig. 38 Understanding parenting advantage.

In combination these concepts form the foundation of the corporate strategy

These two concepts fit together neatly in the grid below (see Figure 39). Plotting the current and potential business in this grid creates a powerful set of static hypotheses about what the business might do. It is also possible to use the grid to create dynamic hypotheses addressing the issue of moving a business from one cell to another – for example, if you had a sufficiently interesting business in the top left cell, it might be worth assessing the chances of reinventing the corporation so as to become a good parent for this business, rather than just selling it to one who is currently a better parent.

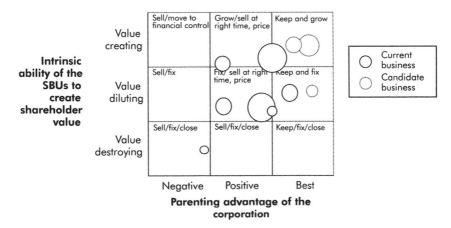

Fig. 39 The foundation of corporate strategy.

These hypotheses start to give a clear picture of all the actions the parent can take to create value:

• Which businesses to buy

• Which to sell

• How to intervene to add most value to those in the portfolio.

In most cases, the hypotheses you create will cause you to face 'bet-the-ranch' decisions, and the techniques set out in Part 4 should be applied to ensure that your decisions are the right ones.

In summary

By combining the ideas of the rest of this book with the concepts of parenting characteristics, parenting actions and parenting advantage, you can analyze the corporation and develop the key hypotheses you need to maximize corporate value. The techniques set out in the CEO's toolkit will help you test these hypotheses and create a powerful value-based corporate strategy.

Appendix 2: Value measurement

In this book we have talked extensively about value creation as the over-arching goal for a CEO. This appendix will explain the three measures of value used in this book, albeit in a slightly more technical manner than the earlier sections. These three measures are:

- Intrinsic value (IV), the current value of the business based on its future cash generation

- Total shareholder return (TSR), the return an investor would get by holding shares in a business

- Economic profit (EP), the profit generated by the business adjusted for the cost of capital employed.

This appendix will also show that these measures are consistent with each other, being in fact different perspectives on the same thing, and that a CEO's objective can be to maximize value according to any of these measures.

The measures and their relationships to each other are explained in more detail below.

Intrinsic value

In the *Owners' Manual*, his booklet for Berkshire Hathaway investors, Warren Buffet defines the intrinsic value of a business as the 'discounted value of the cash that can be taken out ... during its remaining life'. Thus we are able to express intrinsic value as:

$$IV = NPV(CF)$$

where CF represents the stream of future cash flows to equity holders, sometimes referred to as long-term shareholder value. The rate at which cash flows are discounted is called the cost of equity.

Total shareholder return and intrinsic value

We are able to show that IV maximization is equivalent to maximization of TSR, by showing that any increase in IV results in an increase in TSR.

This relies on three fundamental assertions:

- If a business is correctly valued, then its market value (MV) will be equal to its IV

- The purchase of shares at a correctly valued MV is a zero NPV transaction

- The TSR on a correctly valued share is equal to the cost of equity.

The first assertion arises because the MV of a correctly valued company is the value that a rational investor places on the future cash flows from the business, and is thus no different from our definition of IV.

Unfortunately, we know that valuations of future cash flows are difficult and that not all investors are rational, and thus MV does not always equal IV, but that does not affect this argument.

The second assertion follows simply from the first because, as shown below, the initial cash flow ($CF1^*$) corresponding to a purchase of shares at an MV equal to IV will exactly equal the value of the cash flows after that point (see Figure 40).

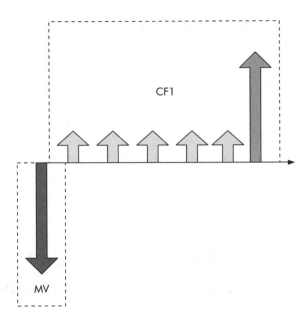

Fig. 40 In a perfect model the market value (MV) should exactly equal the future value of the cashflows (CF1).

Mathematically:

$$NPV(CF1^*) = NPV(CF1) - MV$$

However, for a correctly valued company:

$$MV = IV = NPV(CF1)$$

And thus:

$$NPV(CF1^*) = NPV(CF1) - NPV(CF1) = 0$$

i.e. buying shares at intrinsic value is a zero NPV transaction.

Reconsidering the transaction shown above we are able to see that, at an NPV of zero, the resulting stream of returns arising are exactly equal to the cost of the equity employed in order to obtain these returns. Thus, recalling the definition of TSR as the internal rate of return over this pattern of cash flows, we are able to see that the TSR of a zero NPV transaction is equal to the cost of equity, our third assertion.

Put most simply, if the share is *not* correctly valued then:

- If it is overvalued, the future TSR will be below the cost of equity

- If it is undervalued, the future TSR will be above the cost of equity.

These results accord with common sense, which says that it is better to buy an undervalued share than an overvalued one.

Raising intrinsic value will raise future TSR

The future TSR on the strategy shown above (which would give rise to cash flows CF1), given a share purchased at the original intrinsic value, is simply the cost of equity. If an alternative strategy (which would give rise to cash flows CF2) raises the IV, so that NPV(CF2) > NPV(CF1) and so that IV is now greater than MV, and if we define CF2* as CF2 extended with the actual purchase price of the share, then we would have:

$$NPV(CF2^*) = NPV(CF2) - MV$$

But

$$MV = NPV(CF1)$$

So

$$NPV(CF2^*) = NPV(CF2) - NPV(CF1) > 0, \text{ since } NPV(CF2) > NPV(CF1).$$

The TSR for CF2*, i.e. the internal rate of return on CF2*, must therefore be higher than Ke (because for cash flows of this type, NPV decreases as the discount rate increases). Raising the intrinsic value has therefore raised the future TSR. (Of course, anyone buying at the *new* intrinsic value will still only get Ke as a return.)

We have now shown that increasing the intrinsic value is equivalent to raising TSR. Two of the three measures are consistent: this just leaves EP to consider.

Increasing IV is equivalent to increasing the future stream of EP

There is a simply expressed mathematical link between EP and IV:

IV = Book Value + NPV(EP1)

where EP1 represents the future stream of economic profit corresponding to the cash-flow stream CF1. This link holds as long as flow-through accounting is used – i.e. as long as:

Profit After Tax – (change in Book Value) = Cash flow to equity

The link means that the future EP stream accounts for the difference between book value and intrinsic value – i.e. the value created above what investors have put in. It also, of course, means that any strategy that increases the value of the future stream of EP will increase intrinsic value.

We have seen that increasing one of these measures is equivalent to increasing the other two – in other words, a business that aims to maximize long-term shareholder value is maximizing:

- Intrinsic value

- Future TSR

- The future stream of EP.

The different measures meet different needs

This tempts one to say, 'Why all these measures?' In fact, although they are equivalent in the sense described above, they have distinct uses (see Figure 41).

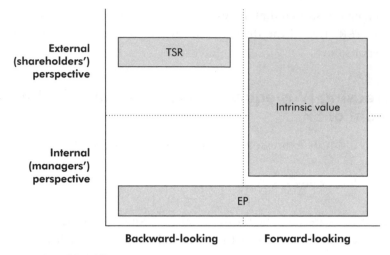

Fig. 41 Roles of the different measures.

Figure 41 draws two distinctions: between backward-looking and forward-looking measures, and between the shareholders' and the managers' perspectives. It also illustrates how the measures relate to the four resulting combinations.

Shareholders are interested in knowing:

- For shares they hold: 'Has this been a good investment?' – for which purpose TSR is the most appropriate measure

- For shares they are thinking of buying (or selling): 'Is this share over- or under-valued?' – for which intrinsic value is the key measure.

Managers are interested in the above, of course, but more directly, for managing the business, they need to know the answers to questions like:

- 'Was this a good quarter?' 'Are we making money in China?' 'Is the new model profitable yet?' – for all of which, EP is the simplest measure

- 'Which strategy will create more value?' 'Should we go for smaller volumes but higher margins in the up-market segment, or aim to get a large share of the mass-market?' – for which intrinsic value or the future stream of EP are appropriate measures.

In conclusion, the different measures are consistent ways of taking a different view of the same thing: long-term shareholder value.

Index